Area Man Says:

Flying Saucer Spotted in 1933

Flying saucers have been reported by persons in all walks of life all over the world, including the Lehigh Valley. About 30 years ago a Lehigh Valley man claims he actually entered and inspected a saucer at close hand. Mr. X's identity has been withheld to protect him from hecklers but his story is recounted here.

Early on a warm summer morning — actually about 2:30 a.m. in 1933 — I was on my way to Nazareth from Lehighton. I was driving a 1925 Ford roadster.

Between Cherryville and Morrestown at a lonely spot on the road one of my tires went flat.

While jacking up the car, I noticed a faint violet or purplish light in the field on my right. It was not especially bright but the peculiarity of the hue made me curious.

Bell-Shaped Object

I walked about 200 feet toward the light. On the grass lay a bell-shaped object about ten feet in diameter and about six feet high.

There was no moon but a faint light emanated from the stars. Light was also issuing from a slit in the object which proved to be a circular door, slightly ajar, on close examination.

This door was about a foot in diameter. When I pushed it, it swung open. It was constructed somewhat like a bank vault door with sealing steps on its edges and at the opening.

There was nobody around so I put my head inside. But, because of the peculiar light —apparently coming from the ceiling—I had difficulty seeing.

Tubing and Dials

The chamber was full of tubing and dials with a kind of console in the center. There were no perceivable windows. The chamber was about six feet in diameter and about four feet high and it had a dome.

The Morning Call (Allentown, PA.)
2-16-1964, p. 17

Photo of a UFO Taken on 9-14-1931

UFOS OF THE TURBULENT THIRTIES

AMERICAN SIGHTINGS

1930-1939

By Noe Torres & John LeMay

ROSWELL BOOKS.COM

Roswell, New Mexico · Edinburg, Texas

Cover Illustration by Jolyon Yates

Torres, Noe.
LeMay, John.
   UFOs of the Turbulent Thirties:
   American Sightings, 1930-1939
     1.   History—1930s. 2. Ufology—Study of
        Unidentified Flying Objects. 3. Folklore, early
        day America.

Noe Torres: For Dad, who worked difficult jobs as a construction worker and farm laborer to keep his family fed. He sacrificed so that I could have a better life, and I never properly thanked him for all he did for me.

John LeMay: For Fred Boggs, thanks for all you do for the Historical Society for Southeast New Mexico!

ACKNOWLEDGMENTS

Thanks to Dr. John Stamey and Devin Tait of ScaryCast for their help uncovering the lost Lizard City of Los Angeles.

PREFACE

AS EVERY DEDICATED UFO enthusiast knows, in June of 1947, Kenneth Arnold spotted a fleet of UFOs which the news media referred to as "flying saucers". This essentially kicked off what would later be called the "Golden Age of Flying Saucers," a time when the possibility of life on other worlds came to the forefront of the American consciousness. But, as our series of books about UFO cases before 1940 has long strived to emphasize, people the world over had been seeing strange things in the sky long before Kenneth Arnold. What makes this book of particular interest to us is that it explores ufology through the lens of one of the last thoroughly unexplored decades: the Great Depression Era of the 1930s.

In the previous decade, mankind had finally moved past the mysterious airship sightings of the Victorian Era, during which unidentified, highly advanced dirigibles were seen, piloted by humanoids. In the 1920s, as humans took to the air in airplanes, the first mid-air sightings of UFOs surfaced. People flying in planes encountered strange craft in the skies rather than simply sighting them from afar on the ground below. The craft they saw no longer looked like airships or dirigibles. These mysterious craft of the 1920s were often closer to the typical flying saucers that became popular in the 1940s.

Orson Wells, center, explains to the press that the Broadcast was not meant to deceive and frighten listeners as badly as it did.

Of course, many people were too preoccupied with the Great Depression and the horrible dust storms—later termed the Dust Bowl—to be overly concerned about life on other planets. However, though the idea of aliens may not have been a major concern for many U.S. residents in the late 1930s, during Halloween of 1938, something very interesting happened.

On Sunday, October 30, 1938, over the Columbia Broadcasting System radio network, actor Orson Wells narrated a live adaptation of H.G. Wells's *The War of the Worlds*. Though the performance was preceded by a disclaimer that the radio drama was fiction, some listeners missed the introduction. It also didn't help that the "play" was presented as though it was a series of actual radio news broadcasts. These "news bulletins" sporadically interrupted the station's normal music programming with reports of strange happenings across the U.S. The "bulletins" told of odd explosions observed on Mars, followed by a report about an object falling from outer space onto a farm in Grover's Mill, New Jersey. Later, after a musical interlude, the "news" continued with a live report from Grover's Mill, where police officials and a crowd of curious onlookers surrounded the strange craft, which soon disgorged terrifying alien creatures bent on destroying the Earth. The panic over an invasion of hostile aliens had begun!

A considerable number of Americans believed that the "news reports" on the radio were real. The radio broadcast did cause public hysteria in certain regions of the country. It got so out of hand, that the police actually barged into the radio studio where the play was being performed in hopes of shutting down the program.

Producer John Houseman recalled

The following hours were a nightmare. The building was suddenly full of people and dark-blue uniforms. Hustled out of the studio, we were locked into a small back office on another floor. Here we sat incommunicado while network employees were busily collecting, destroying, or locking up all scripts and records of the broadcast. Finally, the Press was let loose upon us, ravening for horror. How many deaths had we heard of? (Implying they knew of thousands.) What did we know of the fatal stampede in a Jersey hall? (Implying it was one of many.) What traffic deaths? (The ditches must be choked with corpses.) The suicides? (Haven't you heard about the one on Riverside Drive?) It is all quite vague in my memory and quite terrible.

The incident wasn't as bad as the sensational press made it out to be at the time, but people were most certainly upset, and much of the night was spent answering angry phone calls and reassuring listeners that the broadcast was a realistic radio play meant to frighten listeners over Halloween, only it had worked a little too well.

This incident very adequately sets the stage for the stories told in this book, wherein we discover that the United States, already on edge over the prospect of another World War, was also becoming increasingly nervous about an invasion from outer space!

The previous decade had proven that humans could fly in aircraft – so why not the inhabitants of other worlds? The reports of strange aircraft that were not of human origin proliferated around the globe in the 1930s, culminating in the beginning of the "Golden Age of Flying Saucers."

As we know, art imitates life, and the pulp literature of the 1930s is full of stories about humans encountering extraterrestrial entities. Science fiction, as popular literature in America, got its start in the pages of pulp magazines such as *Astounding Stories* (first published in January 1930), science fiction's premier publication starting in the 1930s and continuing all the way to the 1970s. Suddenly, the pages of these inexpensive and widely read magazines were filled with stories of space travel, extraterrestrials, life on other planets, and attempts by hostile aliens to take over the Earth. To what extent these stories reflected the UFO sightings that were being reported throughout North America is unknown; however, it is clear that at no previous time in American history had tales of aliens from outer space been so widely available.

For the many people who might have believed that flying saucer sightings began in the 1940s, this book is designed to prove otherwise. Not only were UFOs seen in the skies over North America in the

1930s, but they were seen in astonishingly large numbers!

Astounding Stories Magazine from May 1932.

CONTENTS

ACKNOWLEDGMENTS   vi

PREFACE   vii

Alleged 1939 Photo of a Nazi-Engineered Saucer-Shaped Craft

DID UFOS CAUSE WORLD WAR II?

Germany
1933-1939

AS THE 1930S BEGAN, Americans were for the most part blissfully ignorant of an imminent danger that was rising in Europe and would soon engulf the world, eventually claiming the lives of between 70 and 85 million people, or 3 percent of the world's population. The rise to power of the Nazis in Germany in the 1930s is normally viewed as the coming to power of bloodthirsty thugs and criminals. That they were killers and committed untold atrocities is beyond question, but in the midst of their madness, the Nazis had certain underlying viewpoints and beliefs that caused them to act the way they did, and, incredibly, some of these theories involved extraterrestrials. The net effect of their beliefs caused them to view themselves as "superior" to all the other people on Earth. Conversely, they considered all humans outside their group as "inferior" and worthy of death. Non-Aryans were the "lesser breeds."

Adolf Hitler in 1938

By Bundesarchiv, Bild 183-H12704 / CC-BY-SA 3.0, CC BY-SA 3.0 de,

https://commons.wikimedia.org/w/index.php?curid=5433943

Among a number of paranormal theories the Nazis embraced was the notion that their so-called "Aryan race" was descended from extraterrestrials who had arrived on Earth eons ago. As descendants of aliens, they viewed themselves as having a special destiny that set them clearly apart from all other races and belief systems on the planet.

As Americans watched in horror over the course of the decade of the thirties, the Nazi Terror grew in magnitude and scope, with the German armies marching forward, supremely confident of their superior position over all other lesser breeds.

Although the U.S. did not join the fray until two years later, World War II officially began on September 1, 1939, when the Nazis invaded Poland, causing Great Britain and France to declare war against them.

It was decades after the war ended that documents and witness accounts began to paint a picture of a military regime that was enamored of the supernatural and eager to discover the esoteric secrets of their extraterrestrial ancestors, including space travel. Other paranormal topics they pursued, according to the *Washington Post*, were "the Holy Grail, witchcraft, Luciferianism, World Ice Theory, anti-gravity machines, astrology and pagan religions." Other researchers claim they also delved into inter-dimensional travel and time travel.

Some researchers have suggested that Nazi Germany's interest in the occult and extraterrestrials was a natural extension of its connections to the mysterious secret society known as the Thule. In the article "Adolf Hitler and Nazis were in touch with aliens, shock claims" in England's *Daily Star*, the following is revealed:

Researchers claim senior members of the Thule Society believed a master race of alien beings were living in underground caverns – right here on Earth.

This subterranean society – called the Vril-ya – was said to have developed futuristic technology far beyond the reach of humans, including a liquid energy source known as "Vril".

Vril could power machines and heal living creatures. But it also had awesome destructive power – such that a couple of Vril-ya could easily wipe out an entire city. [https://www.dailystar.co.uk/news/weird-news/thule-society-vril-nazi-ufos-20698794]

The *Daily Star* further says, "Nazi Germany was developing a mysterious range of futuristic aircraft towards the end of World War 2 – some of which looked suspiciously like UFOs. UFO hunters have suggested these Nazi flying saucers were fueled by Vril or other extra-terrestrial technology."

Some believe that a series of UFO sightings in Eastern Europe in the 1930s led Nazi scientists to become even more interested in UFOs, hoping to somehow exploit alien technology to gain power over the other nations of the world. They say this belief led to the Nazis embarking on many efforts to invent technologies of a kind never before known to mankind, including rockets, saucer-shaped aircraft, and more.

Among the UFO cases that reportedly inspired the Nazis was the controversial, alleged crash of an extraterrestrial spacecraft in Schwarzwald (Black Forest) near Freiburg in 1936. Some researchers have claimed that the Germans were able to advance their war technologies by carefully studying the wreckage of the UFO. Although this story is hotly disputed and may be entirely false, the rise of Nazi Germany and its high-tech war machine, coming upon the heels of their bitter defeat in World War I, is nothing short of amazing. It almost seems as though they found a "shortcut" to advancing their technology in an incredibly brief span of time.

German Physicist Hermann Oberth

After the war, Nazi scientist Hermann Oberth, considered the father of the Nazi rocket program, made a series of puzzling statements, including: "We cannot take credit for our record advancement in certain scientific fields alone. We have been helped, and we have been helped by the people of other worlds." This help that Oberth refers to came by contacting extraterrestrials via "channeling," a process where spirit beings take over a human body and communicate by the human's vocal cords. Oberth himself was a psychic medium that believed he was in contact with extraterrestrials.

About UFOs, Oberth said, "It is my thesis that flying saucers are real and that they are spaceships from another solar system. There is no doubt in my mind that these objects are interplanetary craft of some sort. I and my colleagues are confident that they do not originate in our solar system."

Throughout Europe, in the 1930s, were many other astonishing UFO sightings that surely caught the attention of the Germans, such as one that happened in New Forest, England, on July 14, 1934. Paul Faiveley, a French tourist, was standing outside his rented cabin, when he noticed that the ground all around him was illuminated brightly. Looking up, he saw a "perfectly circular disc of a vivid white color" that was too bright to look at directly.

When Faiveley first saw the object, it was moving, but afterward, the object stopped and hovered above him. "After about two minutes or so," he said, "the machine, which lit up the whole countryside around, developed a blue fringe around it, like a halo, concentric to the dazzling white circle."

Moments later, the blue light "winked" out, and the brilliant white light became dimmer, then turned yellow, orange, and red. Suddenly, the object took off at great speed, vanishing in seconds. The incident was reported in Jerome Clark's *The UFO Encyclopedia*.

Most likely because of their research into these and other strange sightings, Nazi scientists started experimenting with saucer shaped craft, perhaps as early as 1939. In his book *The Flying Saucers Are Real*, author Donald Keyhoe interviewed an aeronautical engineer that was familiar with the Nazi experiments regarding flying disks. Here is what the engineer told Keyhoe:

"I can tell you a little more," he said. "Some top Nazi scientists were convinced we were being observed by space visitors. They'd searched all the old reports. Some sighting over Germany set them off about 1940. That's what I was told. I think that's where they first got the idea of trying out oval and circular airfoils.

"Up to then, nobody was interested. The rotation idea uses the same principle as the helicopter, but nobody had even followed that through. The Nazis went to work on the disks. They also began to rush space-exploration plans--the orbiting satellite idea. I think they realized these spaceships were using some great source of power we hadn't discovered on earth. I believe that's what they were after--that power secret. If they'd succeeded, they'd have owned the world. As it was, that space project caused them to leap ahead of everybody with rockets."

Although many of the Nazi's secret efforts to create advanced, esoteric technologies were not pursued in earnest until the 1940s, they were already working on rockets as early as 1934. Nazi rocket scientist Werner Von Braun was busily engaged in helping Germany develop the technology, successfully launch-testing two rockets in 1934. Yes, he was the same Von Braun that later created America's space program and became director of the National Aeronautics and Space Administration (NASA).

As the tide of war seemed to be turning more and more against them, the Nazis intensified their efforts to create an entire range of highly advanced "wonder weapons," which they called *wunderwuffe*. A number of these weapons – including the V-2 rockets, advanced fighter planes, and powerful bombs – were successfully developed, but many other weapons remained in the planning stages at the time that the war ended.

Nazi Scientist Werner Von Braun

Among the projects that never got off the ground were missiles and bombers capable of reaching the United States from Germany, submarines that could launch V-2 rockets from off the U.S. coast, an orbital space platform that could focus the sun's energy to destroy a city, anti-gravity propulsion, saucer-shaped aircraft, and much more. While the concepts were amazing, the raw materials and manufacturing techniques of the 1930s and 1940s did not lend themselves to such advanced designs. To a certain extent, it was like handing a modern cell phone to someone in the 1800s and asking them to manufacture copies of it – the pattern to make it was there, but the tools, know-how, and raw materials were not.

Nazi Concept for Transatlantic Bomber Plane –
the Horten H.XVIII

As stated before by Oberth, the concepts for these highly advanced weapons were given to the Nazis by "the people of other worlds" via channeling by medium. Decades later, many of these weapons finally saw the light of day after captured Nazi scientists continued working on them in the United States, Russia, and other countries, where they were taken after the war. The technological ideas of the Nazi scientists were mind blowing, although most of these concepts did not materialize until decades later.

Nazi Concept for a Long-Range Bomber Capable of Reaching the U.S.

Historian Michael J. Neufeld has said that "the net result of all these weapons, deployed or otherwise, was that the Reich wasted a lot of money and technical expertise (and killed a lot of forced slave laborers) in developing and producing exotic devices that yielded little or no tactical and strategic advantage." But what if the Nazi's had had more time and access to more raw materials and better manufacturing techniques?

Historians are convinced that if Nazi Germany had a few more years, they would have achieved technological mastery over all other nations on Earth. They would have more fully developed rockets; they would have created atomic bombs; and it's likely they would have perfected a few other advanced technologies.

LONG SEARCH MADE FOR AIRPLANE IN SOUTH BRUNSWICK

Garage Owner Says He Saw Plane Drop After Flying Low Over Pike

NO NEARBY PLANES REPORTED MISSING

Central New Jersey Home News, 12-30-1932, p. 1.

THE MYSTERIOUS "GHOST FLYERS"

The U.S. and Europe
1932-1939

FROM 1932 TO 1939, a very strange aerial phenomena occurred in various places around the globe, involving the appearance of enigmatic, unidentified aircraft that were called "Ghost Flyers" or "Mystery Airplanes." In his book *Alien Encounters: True-Life Stories of UFOs and Other Extra-Terrestrial Phenomena*, British author Rupert Matthews describes them in this manner: "When seen in daylight, the ghost fliers took the form of extremely large aircraft, bigger than anything then flying, colored grey and without markings of any kind. At night the aircraft often shone dazzlingly bright searchlights down to the ground. The ghost fliers usually came alone, but sometimes appeared in groups of two or three."

UFOs OF THE TURBULENT THIRTIES

Although most cases occurred in Northern Europe, a few cases were also reported in the United States, as will be discussed in this chapter. The U. S. cases were much fewer in number and did not receive as much media attention as those in Europe.

Of the European sightings, Matthews wrote, "These odd aircraft were seen hundreds of times over Finland, Sweden, and Norway between 1932 and 1937.... At first the various Scandinavian governments thought that they were being overflown by top secret scout aircraft from Russia, Germany, or Britain. It soon became clear, however, that the ghost fliers were performing aerobatics and achieving speeds utterly impossible to any known aircraft – and, with hindsight, impossible even today."

Similarly, the handful of sightings that occurred over North America also caused a lot of consternation. Military officials wondered what agencies were engaged in flying these sophisticated aircraft at their leisure all over the nation. To a certain extent, the phenomenon seemed very similar to the airship sightings of 1896 and 1897, except these craft resembled airplanes, rather than airships.

As we have stated previously, if extraterrestrials were trying to attract as little attention as possible, it would be advantageous for them to disguise their craft to make them appear to be manmade ships. Since manmade airships were becoming more common in the late 1800s, the ETs would logically make their craft look like airships. And when airplanes began soaring overhead in the early 1900s, the ETs would undoubtedly make their vessels appear to be airplanes, albeit not exactly similar.

"GHOST FLYERS" OF NORWAY

Mystery Aeroplane

COPENHAGEN, FEBRUARY 7.

For the past two months speculation has been rife regarding the nationality and the purpose of the mysterious aeroplanes which fly night by night over the northern parts of Norway, Sweden, and Finland.

The mysterious aeroplanes have become known as "the ghost flyers." Among the speculations which have been made is the suggestion that the airmen are Russians and are practising night flying. This, however, has been officially denied by the Soviet.

Another suggestion is that the flyers are Japanese operating from a vessel which more than once has been seen off the coast.

Yesterday news came from Norway which it was hoped would lead to a solution of the mystery. One of the machines was reported to have made a forced landing on the plateau on the top of Mount Fagerfjeld, near Tromsol.

The local sheriff and the military authorities sent out an expedition, but by the time the party reached the mountain darkness had set in and it had to return. This morning further expeditions were dispatched, prepared for all eventualities, but a blinding snowstorm impeded their progress. Altogether three parties were sent out before the plateau was reached. They all returned in an exhausted condition this evening.

They reported that some 300 to 400 yards from the spot where the aeroplane was said to have alighted they came across parallel lines in the snow, which had presumably been made by aeroplane skis. The frozen snow along the lines had been crushed as if a great weight had passed over it. Also there were footmarks as made by two men. Of the aeroplane itself there was no sign. The mystery, therefore, is a mystery still.—Exchange Telegram.

The Guardian (London), 2-8-1934, p. 9.

As pointed out by Matthews, the Ghost Fliers looked like large airplanes but "were performing aerobatics and achieving speeds utterly impossible to any known aircraft." Even today's aircraft would be unlikely to reproduce the maneuvers and velocity exhibited by these mystery craft of the 1930s.

An article on *UFOcasebook.com* describes even more amazing capabilities: "They were never seen to land, had no markings, and were seen to operate at low altitude in weather conditions (such as heavy snow) which would seem to have been nearly impossible for aircraft of that era, given the primitive deicing and instrument navigation technology of the time. Furthermore, they did strange things, such as circle in one location for extended periods, shine bright spotlights down upon the ground, and seem to stay aloft even when engine noise ceased. At least some of the accounts described aircraft with as many as eight engines, which is very striking...."

A Russian Tupolev ANT-20 Maxim Gorky – the Largest Airplane of the 1930s

Skeptics have proposed that the mystery airplanes seen in Europe might have been the mammoth, eight-engine Tupolev ANT-20 airplane, which was the largest plane in the world of the 1930s. However, due to the amazing maneuvers carried out by the mystery planes, it seems unlikely that the ANT-20 would have been able to fit the bill.

More information about the mystery craft appears in the Finnish version of *Wikipedia*: "Ghost Airplanes (Ghost Fliers) were observed mainly in the 1930s, mostly in the north in Finland, Sweden and Norway.... Observations were also made in other parts of the world, including Britain and the United States .... The planes often had floodlights aimed at the ground, they flew in very dangerous weather, made incredible flight maneuvers, and displayed no markings. They often operated in snowstorms and in fog. In many cases, the airplane's cockpit was brightly lit.

"The planes often flew dangerously low or hovered in the air in place. They could sound like a normal plane or be completely silent. Their maneuvering was way beyond the norm, and there were no known accidents. Of the many sightings, crew were rarely seen, although once, two white-fur men were seen in the brightly lit cockpit of the plane."

One of the more interesting "Mystery Airplane" sightings in the United States occurred on the Connecticut shore of Long Island Sound, near the Byram River, in 1932 or 1933. The two eyewitnesses did not report the incident until many years later and could not remember the exact date.

The witnesses, who were standing facing to the southeast, had observed several conventional aircraft flying over the Sound when they suddenly noticed something in the air that was completely unlike the normal airplanes. This object was moving much faster, and as it passed them on their right side, it suddenly made a sharp turn to the left into the rays of the setting sun, passing directly above them at great speed.

The object was described as "cigar-shaped, emitting a pink glow at its front and a light swirl of grey smoke along its sides." It was huge compared to any other plane, and it had no rudder, wings, or elevator.

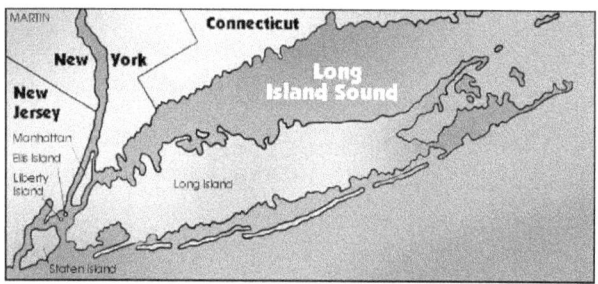

The Area of the Sighting

As the amazed witnesses continued to watch, the strange craft disappeared off to the Northwest, seemingly headed to a point between Rye (N.Y.) and Port Chester (N. Y.).

Another remarkable "Mystery Airplane" case occurred in New Jersey in December of 1932, when witnesses stated that a tri-motor plane with a large passenger cabin flew overhead at night and seemed to crash-land nearby. An all-out search was conducted the following day to no avail. The newspaper story about the incident stated:

A search which continued throughout the night and up until noon today had failed to reveal any trace of an airplane which was reported to have crashed in the vicinity of the Margo Inn, eight miles west of this city on the Brunswick pike in South Brunswick Township last night.

The report of the accident emanated from Tony Traficante of 29 Redmond Street, proprietor of a garage on the pike near Monmouth Junction. Traficante said he was on his way from his garage to the Margo Inn to get a cup of coffee end had stopped his car momentarily about a quarter of a mile west of the inn when he saw a large plane circling down, its motors off and cabin lights blinking.

Thinking that the apparently distressed pilot might try to land his craft on the highway, Traficante said he jumped into his car and moved it to give ample room for the plane to light.

As he did so, Traficante said, the plane veered to the south, and appeared to be about to crash directly back of the Margo Inn.

The witness said he could hear the sound of the wind whistling through the struts of the plane as it zoomed over the highway but did not hear any sound of a crash as his motor was running at the time.

The plane appeared to have been headed in the direction of Newark, he said. Traficante's first move was to circle the area within which he thought the craft had crashed, hoping to locate it and render assistance to the occupants. After completing his circuit, which took him back as far as Monmouth Junction, without finding any trace of the fallen plane, Traficante stopped at Spilatore's garage, a mile east of the Margo Inn at Sand Hill, where he picked up Anthony Spilatore.

Traficante and Spilatore contacted the local airports to check on missing planes but were told that all airplanes were accounted for. And thus came to an end another mysterious airplane sighting in the U.S.

Another puzzling case of a mystery airplane occurred off the coast of North America on the evening of July 21, 1937. The newspaper headlines proclaimed, "Mysterious Airplane Seen Far Out at Sea by Atlantic Steamer."

The master of a British freighter steaming through the north Atlantic reported to the Radio Marine corporation tonight the passage of a mysterious airplane, heading east. The steamer, the 5,000-ton Ranee, was then 500 miles off Cape Race, Newfoundland. If the pilot of the unidentified aircraft was some unknown [person] undertaking an ocean flight to Europe he or she faced more than 1,500 miles of open water.

Surprised members of the freighter crew reported hearing the roar of the plane's motor, or motors, as it passed swiftly overhead, and said they caught a brief view of its running lights, gleaming brightly against the sky.

But, said a radio message from the ship, its crew was unable to determine the size of the aircraft, or whether it was land or seaplane.

Government radio stations stood by tonight along Canada's eastern coast for some word from the mysterious flyer. The Canadian press said a check showed that no plane took off from the landing fields usually used by those trying the Atlantic venture. Authorities at St. Johns, N. F., scene of the take-off of both the Pan-American Clipper III and the Imperial Airways flying boat Caledonia on trans - Atlantic crossings, within the last two weeks said no airplane had taken off tonight from Newfoundland.

Transport department officials of the Canadian government at Ottawa said they had no recent requests for permission to make a flight over or from Canada.

Pan-American Airways said the plane was not one of the trans-Atlantic survey planes used by Pan-American and Imperial (British) Airway in charting a new air route to Europe.

Coast Guard headquarters here said none of the Coast Guard's ocean-going patrol planes was in the vicinity of Cape Race.

The mystery of the "Ghost Flyers" began to taper off in 1937 and seemed to end completely in 1939, just as World War II fired up in Europe. To this day, these strange aircraft sightings remain as much of a puzzle as they were in the 1930s, again hearkening back to the enigma of the airships during the late 1890s.

Mysterious Airplane Seen Far Out at Sea By Atlantic Steamer

NEW YORK, July 21.—(*P*)—The master of a British freighter steaming through the north Atlantic reported to the Radio Marine corporation tonight the passage of a mysterious airplane, heading east.

The steamer, the 5,000-ton Ranee, was then 500 miles off Cape Race, Newfoundland. If the pilot of the unidentified aircraft was some unknown undertaking an ocean flight to Europe he—or she—faced more than 1,500 miles of open water.

Tampa Bay (Fla.) Times, 7-22-1937, p. 1

It seems apparent that Nazi scientists, who were very interested in harvesting advanced technology for their war effort, were undoubtedly paying close attention to these puzzling aircraft that were being seen throughout the world in the thirties. Consequently, Nazi Germany came up with a series of unique aircraft designs that, luckily for the rest of the world, were mostly not perfected prior to the end of the World War. It wasn't until many years after the war that researchers realized how perilously close the world came to having the Nazis totally dominate the planet, sparked by their amazing aircraft designs.

THE AMERICAN AUTHOR AND THE REPTILIANS

Texas
1930-1936

THE NAZI BELIEF THAT their culture arose from extraterrestrials was a concept reflected in the fictional writings of American author Robert E. Howard. A native of Texas, Howard gave birth to the idea that an ancient race of extraterrestrials had existed on Earth and that it interfered in human affairs in a clandestine manner. Howard is best known for creating the character of Conan the Barbarian. Although he wrote fiction, his concepts were based on ancient belief systems, some of which were similar to the ideas that were gaining a foothold in Nazi Germany at the same time.

American Writer Robert E. Howard in 1934

Many of Howard's stories concerned the "Great Old Ones," an ancient race of extraterrestrials, as explained in *Wikipedia*: "Lovecraft made frequent references to the 'Great Old Ones,' a loose pantheon of ancient, powerful deities from space who once ruled the Earth and have since fallen into a deathlike sleep."

Howard was also one of the first writers to suggest that extraterrestrials resembling reptiles could take the form of human beings and secretly work to bring about the downfall of humanity. In 1929, Howard wrote a story called "The Shadow Kingdom," in which he first introduced the idea of shape-shifting reptile-like humanoids who infiltrate their way into positions of power in an effort to adversely influence human affairs. Howard's "serpent men" were described as humanoids (with human bodies and snake heads) who were able to imitate humans at will, and who lived in underground passages and used their shape changing and mind-control abilities to infiltrate humanity.

Artist's Conception of a Reptilian Humanoid

Howard's concept is believed by many to have later evolved into the "Reptilian Conspiracy Theory," which was popularized in the late 1990s and early 2000s by British writer David Icke.

UFOs OF THE TURBULENT THIRTIES

Excerpt from Howard's "The Shadow Kingdom":

"Kings have reigned as true men in Valusia," the Pict whispered, "and yet, slain in battle, have died serpents—as died he who fell beneath the spear of Lion-fang on the red beaches when we of the isles harried the Seven Empires. And how can this be, Lord Kull? These kings were born of women and lived as men! This—the true kings died in secret—as you would have died tonight—and priests of the Serpent reigned in their stead, no man knowing."

Kull cursed between his teeth. "Aye, it must be. No one has ever seen a priest of the Serpent and lived, that is known. They live in utmost secrecy."

According to Icke, a primary mission of Reptilians is to constantly work to undermine and destabilize human society by infiltrating world governments and working in secret to cause death and destruction among the masses.

What is fascinating is that the Nazis also believed in a superior race of extraterrestrials that lived underground. As previously noted, "Researchers claim senior members of the Thule Society [precursors of the Nazis] believed a master race of alien beings were living in underground caverns – right here on Earth. This subterranean society – called the Vril-ya – was said to have developed futuristic technology far beyond the reach of humans, including a liquid energy source known as 'Vril.'"

*Howard's Famous Story "The Shadow Kingdom"
Appeared in the August 1929 Edition of Weird
Tales*

Interestingly, even as Robert E. Howard met his demise by his own hand in 1936, the Nazi party was gaining in power and would soon bring about the greatest wave of death and horror ever known to humanity, suggesting that they were carrying forth the agenda of the "serpent men," or Reptilians.

It is, of course, unrealistic to blame shape-shifting Reptilian extraterrestrials for all the bloodthirsty human behavior of the 1930s, and we certainly don't mean to suggest this. However, is it possible that human affairs, in a general sense, were being "guided" by mystical groups such as the Thule Society, whose core purpose was to dominate all the people on the earth, killing as many "lesser breeds" as possible? And could these mystic groups have been, in turn, guided by the Reptilians?

DIE GLOCKE, THE NAZI BELL

Germany
1930s and Beyond

IN THE SUDETEN MOUNTAINS of Poland is the mysterious Wenceslas Mine, which is said to have been the location of another attempt by the Nazis to create a wunderwaffe (wonder weapon) during World War II. As has already been established, the Nazis embraced a set of technology concepts that included extraterrestrial life, nuclear weapons, anti-gravity, orbiting space platforms, digital computers, and more. Given time, they might have reached their goals of world domination and the mass extermination of the "lesser breeds."

NAZI BELL

Alleged Nazi Time Travel Experiment
Zusurs, CC BY-SA 3.0 via Wikimedia Commons

One technology that they are said to have embraced, although it remains unproven and highly controversial, is the *Die Glocke*, or "Nazi Bell," that was supposedly used for anti-gravity experiments and may have had the unsettling side effect of disrupting space-time in the immediate vicinity of the object. Researchers say these experiments were carried out in the vicinity of the Wenceslas Mine in Poland.

Although the idea of the *Die Glocke* seems in keeping with the Nazi's other efforts to discover esoteric scientific truths and develop them into tools of war, the problem with the Nazi Bell is that no actual historical proof or documentation has ever been found to support that it actually existed, whether in physical form or as a concept.

The objection has been made that if the Nazis had succeeded in developing anti-gravity, they certainly would have used it toward the tail end of World War II. But others have argued that the technology may not yet have been perfected and may not have been at a stage where it could function as a weapon.

Artistic Rendition of the Nazi Bell During Experimentation

David Winship, CC BY-SA 3.0, via Wikimedia Commons

Hans Kammler

Nonetheless, the idea remains intriguing that Nazi scientists may have been experimenting with counteracting the force of gravity to lift heavy objects off the ground, and that these experiments may have resulted in the creation of a "rift" in space-time that may have hurled an object forward or backward in time.

The *Die Glocke* experiments were reportedly carried out under the supervision of SS General Hans Kammler. Was responsible for Nazi civil engineering projects and its top-secret weapons programs. He oversaw the construction of various Nazi concentration camps before being put in charge of the V-2 rocket and jet programs near the end of World War II. If the *Die Glocke* really did exist, he would have been the logical person to oversee it.

So, what exactly is the Nazi Bell, what is it made of, and what does it supposedly do? The object is said to be a bell-shaped device made of a thick, heavy metal. The device is approximately 9 feet wide and 12-15 feet high. The inside of the device contains two counter-rotating cylinders that are filled with a "mercury-like substance" of a violet color. This metallic liquid was reportedly codenamed "Xerum 525." When not in use, the liquid was stored in tall, thermos-like flasks about a meter high encased in lead. The experiments also utilized several other materials including *Leichmetall* (light metal), thorium and beryllium peroxides.

The information about the *Die Glocke* comes primarily from Polish author Igor Witkowski, who wrote a book in the year 2000 called *The Truth About the Wonder Weapon.*

Although primarily meant to be an anti-gravity device, rumors persist that the Nazi experiments yielded some unexpected results having to do with a local distortion of space-time. Some have said that a concave mirror on top of the device was able to display "images from the past."

Witkowski claims he obtained his information about the Nazi Bell by reading the transcripts from an interrogation of former Nazi SS Officer Jakob Sporrenberg in 1997. He was shown these documents, but not allowed to copy them or take photos of them, by an unidentified agent of the Polish intelligence services. Witkowski's claims were later amplified by other authors.

Unfortunately, no definitive historical documentation has arisen to substantiate Witkowski's claims about Sporrenberg's revelations in his supposed interrogation.

Nazi SS Officer Jakob Sporrenberg

Another researcher, Nick Cook, has written that the *Die Glocke* emitted strong radiation when activated, an effect that supposedly caused the death of several unnamed scientists and various plant and animal test subjects.

Yet another researcher, Joseph P. Farrell, writes that the device was considered so super-secret that the Nazis, in an effort to hide the project's existence, killed 60 scientists that had worked on the project and buried them in a mass grave. Still others suggest that the research on the Nazi Bell continued after World War II in a secret location outside of Germany.

And then there is the possible connection to the reported crash of a bell-shaped UFO in Kecksburg, Pennsylvania, on December 9, 1965. During the evening hours, a large, brilliant fireball was seen in at least six U.S. states and Ontario, Canada, as it streaked over the Detroit, Michigan - Windsor, Ontario area. Reports of hot metal debris over Michigan and northern Ohio, grass fires, and sonic booms in the Pittsburgh metropolitan area were attributed to the fireball. Some people in Kecksburg (about 30 miles southeast of Pittsburgh) reported that something from the sky had crashed in the woods, causing wisps of blue smoke, vibrations, and a "thump."

From the point of the object crashing, the story deviates based on the source. U.S. Air Force personnel and state troopers said they found "nothing" at the crash site. Eyewitnesses who were in the general area claim that the military found a bell-shaped, or "acorn-shaped," object that was subsequently transported away from the scene on a flatbed trailer, covered by a tarp.

The consensus of witnesses who claimed to have seen the recovered object was that it strongly resembled the so-called Nazi Bell of the 1940s.

This resemblance led to speculation that the *Die Glocke* might have somehow become transported in space-time from Poland in 1944 to Pennsylvania in 1965.

In any event, going back to the Nazi Bell project, what finally happened to it as the World War ended? With the surrender of Nazi Germany on May 7, 1945, not much is known about the final disposition of the *Die Glocke*.

SS General Hans Kammler, who would have overseen the *Die Glocke* project, disappeared at around the time of Germany's surrender. There has been much conjecture regarding his fate, with some saying that he committed suicide by ingesting a cyanide capsule and others claiming his aides shot him dead to prevent his being captured. There was also a report that the United States had made Kammler "an offer," presumably to come to the U.S. along with the German scientists and technicians that had worked on Nazi rockets and other secret programs. Kammler, however, was not inclined to accept the offer, saying they would not get him alive.

In the end, his fate remains a mystery, and rumors persist that he escaped Germany after the war. Some of the more extreme theories suggest that he continued to work on the Nazi Bell concept in a Nazi-friendly nation, such as Brazil.

Did the Nazi Bell every really exist? And if it did, what happened to the technology after the conclusion of World War II? Might the Nazi Bell technology have been responsible for some of the many UFO sightings around the world beginning in the late 1940s? After all, it seems remarkable that UFO sightings exploded immediately after the war.

Area Man Says:

Flying Saucer Spotted in 1933

Flying saucers have been reported by persons in all walks of life all over the world, including the Lehigh Valley. About 30 years ago a Lehigh Valley man claims he actually entered and inspected a saucer at close hand. Mr. X's identity has been withheld to protect him from hecklers but his story is recounted here.

Early on a warm summer morning — actually about 2:30 a.m. in 1933 — I was on my way to Nazareth from Lehighton. I was driving a 1925 Ford roadster.

Between Cherryville a n d Morrestown at a lonely spot on the road one of my tires went flat.

While jacking up the car, I noticed a faint violet or purplish light in the field on my right. It was not especially bright but the peculiarity of the hue made me curious.

Bell-Shaped Object

I walked about 200 feet toward the light. On the grass lay a bell-shaped object about ten feet in diameter and about six feet high.

There was no moon but a faint light emanated from the stars. Light was also issuing from a slit in the object which proved to be a circular door, slightly ajar, on close examination.

This door was about a foot in diameter. When I pushed it, it swung open. It was constructed somewhat like a bank vault door with sealing steps on its edges and at the opening.

There was nobody around so I put my head inside. But, because of the peculiar light —apparently coming from the ceiling—I had difficulty seeing.

Tubing and Dials

The chamber was full of tubing and dials with a kind of console in the center. There were no perceivable windows. The chamber was about six feet in diameter and about four feet high and it had a dome.

The Morning Call (Allentown, PA.)
2-16-1964, p. 17

BELL-SHAPED UFO

Cherryville, Pennsylvania
Summer 1933

UFOS IN THE SHAPE OF A BELL are not extremely common in the annals of history. If the so-called "Nazi Bell" might have travelled forward in time to the year 1965, might not it have also travelled backward in time to, say, 1933? While there may be absolutely no connection to the Nazi Bell at all, this 1933 UFO sighting remains one of the more intriguing of the reports received for this particular year.

The incident occurred at 2:30 a.m. on a warm summer morning in 1933, when the eyewitness, age 18, was driving the 26 miles from Nazareth, Pennsylvania, to Lehighton, Pennsylvania. The witness, who requested his name be withheld, was driving a 1925 Ford Roadster, and had reached a lonely stretch of road between Cherryville and Moorestown when one of his tires went flat.

Getting out of the vehicle and starting to jack it up in order to change the tire, he noticed a faint "violet or purplish" light coming from a field located off to his right. Although not very bright, the light seemed unusual because of its color, causing the witness to become curious about it.

1925 Ford Roadster

Leaving his car, he walked toward the light for about 200 feet, finally coming upon a bell-shaped object that had apparently "landed" in the field. Although there was no moonlight, the stars provided a little illumination. Also, light was issuing from the object's circular door, which was slightly ajar.

The strange object was about 10 feet in diameter and about 6 feet high. Based on the witness' description, it was about the same width as the Nazi Bell, but only about half as tall. The Nazi Bell was said to be approximately 9 feet wide and 12-15 feet high.

The witness approached the landed object and moved toward its circular door, which was about a foot in diameter and constructed somewhat like a bank vault door with sealing steps on its edges and at the opening. Tugging on the door, it swung open all the way, revealing an inner chamber and an extremely bright light source that made it difficult to see what was inside the chamber.

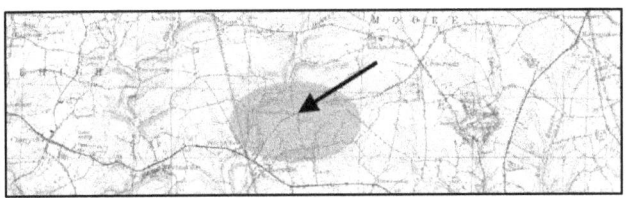

Approximate Area of the UFO Encounter

The witness put his head inside the door opening and noticed that the peculiar violet light was coming from the ceiling of the inner chamber. The chamber was about 6 feet in diameter and about 4 feet high with a dome at the very top. There were no windows or portholes. Around the chamber were a lot of strange tubes and dials, and in the center was a kind of "console."

Looking around the chamber despite the brightness of the ceiling light, the witness noticed the walls had a "striated pattern like that of marble." There were no seats of any kind or anything that could pass for a cot or bed. Since the circular door led directly outside, he guessed there was no airlock.

There was an odor like ammonia present in the chamber, and the temperature was quite cold. He noticed a number of "small objects" scattered around the chamber, none of which seemed familiar and all of which had "strange curves unlike anything I had ever seen before or since."

Pulling his head out of the opening, the witness examined the outside of the object, noticing that the hull was metallic with a very smooth texture and extremely cold to the touch. There were no signs of anybody, human or otherwise, anywhere in the vicinity of the object. Also, he heard absolutely no sound. Although he saw no one, he had the impression that he might have been "observed."

After looking everything over for about ten minutes, the witness fixed his flat tire and left the scene. It was many years before he told his story, at which time he said, "When I had this experience I had never heard of a flying saucer and hadn't the remotest idea what the object was. But now, looking back I am convinced I saw something not of this earth and perhaps not even of our planetary system."

Reflecting further on his experience, the witness added, "I think we of this planet are presumptuous to suppose that all other intelligent beings in the universe have two arms, two legs and look like us. From the size of the door and the odor emanating from the object, it's possible the occupants of this ship were reptilian in nature. And, obviously, judging from its shape, this vehicle propelled by some means other than our clumsy and relatively inefficient rockets."

The witness' guess that the occupants of the ship were "reptilian" is extremely interesting, in the context of the Reptilian Aliens that we have previously discussed, who have been identified by eyewitnesses as one of several species of extraterrestrials that have visited our planet. Of course, due to the small shape of this particular UFO, these Reptilians would have had to be ... well, small.

The area where this encounter happened is about 250 miles from Kecksburg, Pennsylvania, where a Nazi Bell-like object crash-landed in 1965. The fact that the description of this object is generally similar to that of both the Kecksburg object and the Nazi Bell is extremely uncanny.

Jerome Clark, author of *The UFO Encyclopedia*, calls this case "among the most fantastic of pre-1947 UFO reports." Regardless of whether it had any connection whatsoever to the Nazi Bell, it seems to be quite a significant case from the 1930s.

1933 Gangster Mass Murder in Kansas City
(FBI.gov)

GANGSTERS AND ALIENS

North America
1930-1939

LIKE THE NAZIS, America's gangsters and mobsters of the 1930s were cold-blooded murderers who viewed themselves as being above any established societal norms. Like the Nazis, they were often steeped in occult practices, establishing secret societies and practicing arcane rituals. Also like the Nazis, they were following the dictates, consciously or not, of the Reptilian Aliens.

Thus, in this chapter we turn to another source of murder and human misery in the 1930s – the American gangsters and mobsters. These were hardened killers for whom the ends justified all means, including the torture and murder of innocents. Operating in a time of great economic upheaval, with America's Great Depression running from 1929 until nearly 1940, the criminals of the era were motivated by a lust for money and power.

The "gangsters" were generally independent operators who had no allegiance to a larger body of criminals. The "mobsters," as the name implies, were part of a "mob" and operated to fulfill the dictates of the criminal organization to which they belonged. Both were equally ruthless and detrimental to the American public in the thirties.

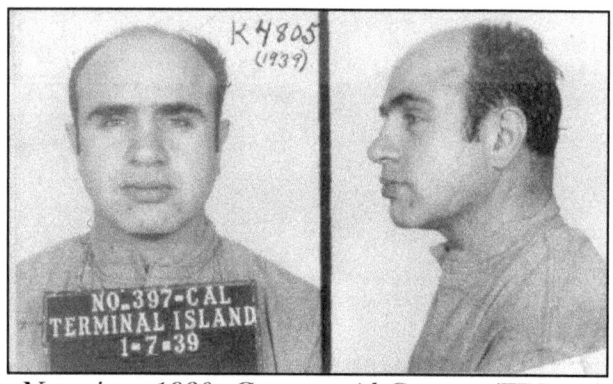

Notorious 1930s Gangster Al Capone (FBI.gov)

Among the most prominent criminals of the 1930s were Al Capone, Bonnie and Clyde, John Dillinger, Baby Face Nelson, Machine Gun Kelly, and Ma Barker. In addition to these, there were many other smaller operators. It was in 1935 that, faced with an alarming increase in lawlessness, the United States government officially created the Federal Bureau of Investigation (FBI), which later became instrumental in investigating UFO cases. Although there were UFOs already popping up all over the country, the fledgling FBI had its hands full with gangsters and was not in a position to look into UFOs until late in the 1940s.

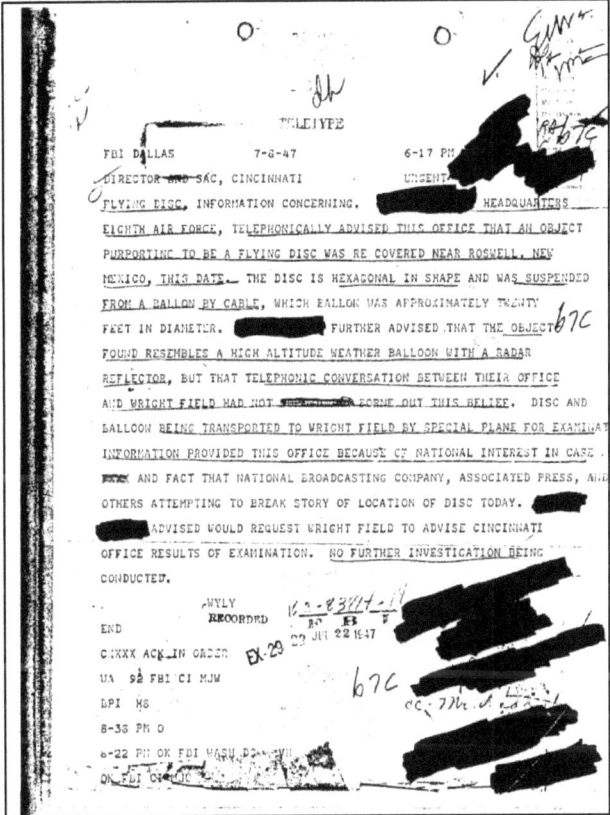

Controversial Memo to FBI Director Herbert Hoover (FBI.gov)

By creating the FBI, America fired a first shot at the Reptilian agenda aimed at bringing terror, chaos, and murder to the nation's citizens. No single man exemplified this "war on terror" better than the FBI's first director, J. Edgar Hoover, an avowed enemy of all criminals, perverts, drug abusers, and subversives. In later years, Hoover also was involved in FBI investigations into UFO cases throughout the land. Perhaps the most controversial UFO document ever released by the FBI was a 1947 memo written to Hoover by FBI special agent Guy Hottel, discussing the alleged recovery of three "flying saucers" in New Mexico.

FBI investigations into UFOs officially began in August 1947 with the dissemination of Bureau Bulletin Number 42, in which Hoover directed, "You should investigate each instance which is brought to your attention of a sighting of a flying disc in order to ascertain whether or not it is a bona fide sighting, an imaginary one or a prank."

This memo from Hoover directly contradicts statements he made at the time and in later years in which he said that the FBI never participated in investigating UFOs. In fact, also in another 1947 document, the FBI confirmed that it had agreed to assist the U.S. Army in its investigation of UFOs, stating "The Bureau, at the request of the Army Air Force Intelligence, has agreed to cooperate in the investigation of flying discs."

Hoover's later attempt to obfuscate the Bureau's role in UFO investigations does not stand up in the wake of all the Freedom of Information document releases regarding UFOs that have been made over the past few years. Hoover not only knew about the investigations but was actively involved in managing them.

7-30-47
BUREAU BULLETIN NO. 42
Series 1947

- 2 -

You should investigate each instance which is brought to your attention of a sighting of a flying disc in order to ascertain whether or not is is a bona fide-sighting, an imaginary one or a prank. You should also bear in mind that individuals might report seeing flying discs for various reasons. It is conceivable that an individual might be desirous of seeking personal publicity, causing hysteria, or playing a prank.

The Bureau should be notified immediately by teletype of all reported sightings and the results of your inquiries. In instances where the report appears to have merit, the teletype should be followed by a letter to the Bureau containing in detail the results of your inquiries. The Army Air Forces have assured the Bureau complete cooperation in these matters and in any instances where they fail to make information available to you or make the recovered discs available for your examination, it should promptly be brought to the attention of the Bureau.

Any information you develop in connection with these discs should be promptly brought to the attention of the Army through your usual liaison channels.

UFOs OF THE TURBULENT THIRTIES

It seems ironic that the war against American gangsters of the 1930s led to the creation of one of the primary UFO investigative bodies, which sprang into action in 1947. Although the two efforts seem totally unrelated, some UFO researchers have suggested that the gangsters were following the same dark agenda that Nazi Germany would soon undertake.

But were there actual connections between America's gangsters and extraterrestrials? While direct evidence is arguably lacking, the gangsters' overall pattern of behavior aligns them with other similar groups carrying out the so-called "Reptilian agenda." By instilling terror and causing murder and mayhem, they were participants in destabilizing human society. Some have even said that their actions revealed that they were under the control of their Reptilian masters.

UFO ENCOUNTER AND MISSING TIME
Texas, 1930

THE CONDON COMMITTEE was a group funded by the U.S. Air Force from 1966 to 1968 at the University of Colorado to study unidentified flying objects under the direction of physicist Edward Condon. After examining hundreds of UFO cases from various sources, the committee issued a much-criticized final report stating that further study of UFOs had no scientific value. Critics say the committee was a final attempt by the U.S. government to "bury" the UFO issue and put to rest all of the public fervor that had been going on since the 1940s.

The Condon committee was highly criticized for shoddy investigative techniques, for failing to follow up with witnesses, for closing investigations without reason, for treating serious cases with flippancy, and more. Unfortunately, the UFO encounter mentioned in this chapter is one that should have received more attention from Condon but was essentially ignored.

Edward Condon

In March 1968, the Condon Committee received a letter from a Texas woman requesting that the committee look into a UFO encounter she had experienced in 1930. She stated in the letter that she had just read *Interrupted Journey*, John Fuller's book about the famous 1961 UFO abduction of Betty and Barney Hill in New Hampshire, in which the Hills suffered lingering physical and emotional problems afterward. In her letter to Condon, the unidentified woman expressed concern that she also had been affected in the same manner as the Hills.

Betty and Barney Hill, 1961
(Courtesy Kathleen Marden)

She insisted that, even though the incident happened 35 years ago she remembered it in great detail. As a result of her encounter, she said, she had been plagued by nervousness and nightmares ever since. Most recently, her doctor had told her family that her "deteriorating health" seemed exacerbated by some type of unresolved stress on her mind. However, she refused to tell anyone about her UFO experience, fearing that they would think she had "lost all my marbles."

According to the witness, she was driving the family car in an isolated hilly area at 10:30 a.m. on a certain day in 1930, although she doesn't remember the exact date. As she went around a curve in the road, she found herself almost directly under a huge UFO that was hovering above the road. In her letter, she said, "It was sort of shiny gun metal color, round and shaped like two dinner plates face-to-face with a dome in the upper top side. It was about 100 feet across, about 15 feet thick. There was a small slender door, and the door chute led down to the ground with steps on the inside of it. The backside of the ship sat on the ground, but the downhill side was braced up with two slender legs with round plates on the ground as feet."

Family Sedan of the 1930s

The next thing she noticed was a man "of normal size" that appeared rather suddenly, walking up to her on the road. She estimated the man to be about 5 feet 10 inches to 6 feet tall and about 165 to 180 pounds. She stated that the man came right up to her and made her feel compelled to talk to him. Strangely, although his mouth and lips were not moving, she could hear him "speaking," which she assumed was telepathy.

Typical Boy Scout Uniform

Suddenly a group of eight to ten smaller humanoids, all dressed in tan uniforms that resembled Boy Scout uniforms, came walking up behind the first person. Interestingly, the newcomers, although of smaller build, did not seem to be children, but rather adults. Also, they had very large, slanted eyes, very large cheekbones, and very thin lips. They seemed to be smiling at her but did not "speak." They seemed to be pushing and jostling each other, as if to get a closer look at her, like kids engaged in horseplay – except they were obviously not kids.

Regarding their appearance, the witness said, "The clothing they wore I at first took to be scout uniforms—tan in color. But when they came up close to me, I saw that there were no pockets, buttons, edges, wrinkles, or pocket flaps. Very clean, neat, and nice. They wore little tight caps cut like baseball caps with little narrow bills. The larger man was dressed the same way. Offhand, the whole bunch seemed like a scoutmaster and his troop of scouts."

Again, without moving his lips, the larger humanoid told her that she would have to move her vehicle off the road, down into a nearby gully, and then back onto the road at a point beyond the landed UFO. "We want the road left clear and open and can't let you through here."

Pointing to the UFO, she asked, "What is that?" But the humanoid ignored the question and reiterated his command for her to get into her car and detour down and around the UFO.

When she objected to pulling her car onto the rock-strewn gully, fearing that it would be damaged, the humanoid told here, "You are a wonderful driver, and you can make it all right."

She responded with uncertainty. "I still griped and argued and said: 'I can't put this big car down through that creek and rocks, it'd tear my car all to pieces, and I could never get out the upper side, and besides you don't own this highway.'"

Despite her misgivings, the woman felt compelled to follow the humanoid's instructions. "... somehow, I couldn't help myself, and dazedly drove very slowly and fearfully down into this creek and rough canyon. I realized that the man was walking right along the side of the car, at my elbow. I felt very safe and was able to make the crossing and was no longer afraid. I wonder why?"

At some point while she was moving the car, she "blanked out." She remembered waking up more than 12 hours later her front porch, located about 15 miles distant from where she saw the UFO. Her vehicle was found parked on the hill beyond the gully, close to where the landed craft had been. She had apparently walked home.

"Where I was, where I went, what happened to me those many hours, I have no idea. Neighbors had driven along that area during the day and told my family that they saw my car parked on the hill beyond the canyon. My dad was forming a search party when I came in."

"That I was taken aboard this saucer and carried away God knows where, I haven't a simple doubt. But, if this did not happen as I remember it, then what did? I want to know so badly that I'm sick. Something did happen - what? I want to know the truth, the whole truth, regardless of what it was."

The Condon Committee, apparently feeling that the letter writer was not in full control of her faculties, took no action whatsoever to check into the incident or to even make contact with the witness to see what could be done to put her mind at ease.

The letter she wrote was filed under the category "psychological," and thus, one of the most fascinating UFO sightings of the 1930s was ignored.

Sightings of strange humanoids during UFO encounters were not unusual in the 1930s, as can be seen from several other reports from this time period.

According to a letter from Mrs. Joy Barish published in *Flying Saucer Review* (Vol. 26 # 6) Cincinnati, Ohio, was the spot of a strange E.T. encounter in 1930.

The letter read:

Dear Sir. — In late 1930s, a friend of mine, who now lives in Michigan, but who was then a resident of Cincinnati, Ohio — a little girl of 8 at the time —picked up what she called a "tiny man" from a rainswept gutter. Her description of it, and the illustration she sent me, was of an elf as described in Geoffrey Hodson's *Fairies at Work and Play.*

She said it had "petrified eyes" and she was all but persuaded to hand it over to a neighbor who regarded her discovery with a cold fish eye. He asked her to give "it" to him, but she let it go and it scampered away between two houses. It had a tight-fitting suit, its face was small and triangular with pointed ears, and slanting eyes too. It was as agile as any insect, but it certainly was not the "praying mantis" the cold-eyed neighbor insisted it might be. Right before she picked up

this tiny entity she saw a balloon-shaped object
fly over hills beyond the city.

That the strange little creature was seen shortly
after what may have been an airship sighting, rather
than a simple balloon as they young girl implied, is
fascinating. In the letter, Mrs. Barith goes on to
relate that the unnamed witness went on to have
nightmares. She wrote that, "For many years after
that she had grotesque nightmares of terrible-
looking creatures dancing in a mad circle behind
her house." Barith also related that the day after
one of the horrible dreams, she went to the spot
behind her house where her dream was set only to
find that "the grass there had been flattened into a
circle and seemed to remain greener than the rest
of the yard."

What Barith related sounds very much like both a classic "fairy ring" and a miniature crop circle. In the very first book of our series, *Early American UFOs*, we detailed some of the startling similarities between crop circles and fairy rings, not to mention the commonalities shared between fairies and aliens.

Our next weird alien encounter takes place in Wayne County, Tennessee, also in the year 1930. One night along a lonely stretch of Beech Creek Road, a man claimed to have seen bright lights emanating from the nearby woods. A bit later, he encountered small men with "wrinkled faces" and "reddish complexions". These tiny humanoids (he didn't give exact measurements or heights) chased the man through the woods. The man became so terrified that he passed out from fright and later awoke in a field. Did he suffer some kind of abduction experience as a result? We don't know, but the encounter was recorded in a publication called *Alternate Perceptions* in the Winter 1995 edition.

Later that summer, in Lisbon, Ohio, more strange humanoids were encountered in broad daylight. Several young people were on their way back from taking a dip in a local swimming hole. As they strolled through the woods, they sighted creatures of a whitish color, which were eerily devoid of discernible facial features. The strange creatures seemed to be scurrying around, and luckily didn't notice them. Years later, when one of the young men reported the sighting, he likened the creatures to the "Shmoos" from the "Lil

Abner" comic strip. These creatures originated in 1948, which means the witness came forward about his sighting years later when UFO sightings began to be reported.

In the fall of that year, strange entities visited Pittsylvania and Virginia. A witness identified only as Collins reported hearing a loud humming sound coming from behind a knoll. The source of the noise turned out to be a large, glowing aluminum-colored domed disc about 70 feet away from where he stood. Out of the craft came beings about 3-½ feet tall, which is close to the size of many alien Greys. However, these beings were wearing green coveralls and helmets. This is actually not all that strange, as sightings of small humanoids wearing green suits of some kind have been reported many times before. A more widely circulated case of a green-suited entity occurred in Texas in either 1913 or 1914, and a pack of farm dogs tore the little creature to pieces.

In this case, the little, green-suited men that Collins observed were busy collecting soil samples, also not unusual as we have come across several cases where witnesses observed beings taking samples of soil and plant life. Eventually, the creatures reboarded their ship and it took off. This sighting was recorded by the reputable Richard Hall in UFOCAT.

MASS ABDUCTION AT ANGIKUNI LAKE
The Yukon
November 1930

THE FROZEN YUKON TERRITORY of North America is no stranger to stories of UFOs and extraterrestrials. Some of the earliest such tales date all the way back to the very early 1800s concerning alien beings in Koyuk, Alaska (near Nome) which we covered in our book *Early American UFOs*. A more recent example of alleged alien encounters in the frozen north that might come to mind in the general public is the movie *The Fourth Kind* (2009). The film was passed off as a docu-drama based upon real events concerning alien abductions in Nome. However, that movie is pure fiction in the style of *The Blair Witch Project* (1999), though it has fooled several people over the years into thinking it was based on real events.

Somewhat similar to the case of the movie is a sensational newspaper article from the year 1930. Like *The Fourth Kind*, it involves a mass disappearance in the frozen north and its authenticity is debatable.

Angikuni_Lake
[wikipedia CC0 Nicolas Perrault III]

Our story begins in late November of 1930 with a trapper named Joe Labelle, on his way to a small Innuit village he had visited before near Angikuni Lake. To his shock, Labelle found the small village of 25 people to be completely deserted. At first, as Labelle spied the familiar village under the light of a full moon, he simply thought everyone was still inside their tents. The only strange thing was he could see no fires going. Labelle then proceeded to look inside of the tents, and to his shock, he found not a single soul there. It wasn't a simple case of the villagers picking up and moving on to a new location. The villagers had left all of their possessions there, including the rest of their food supplies.

In an article on the incident, Labelle related, "I felt immediately that something was wrong... In view of half cooked dishes, I knew they had been disturbed during the preparation of dinner. In every cabin, I found a rifle leaning beside the door and no Eskimo goes nowhere without his gun... I understood that something terrible had happened."

It was as though the residents left in a hurry. Or, if they didn't leave, perhaps they were taken...

Indicating that the village's inhabitants literally disappeared from the face of the earth, Labelle—an experienced tracker—could find no footprints or tracks indicating an exodus from the village. Today, many people have theorized that aliens were to blame. In fact, even Labelle's first thought was along the lines of a being from the sky taking the villagers. However, Labelle was thinking of an evil spirit called Torngarsuk said to come down from the sky rather than aliens, which still weren't embedded in the public consciousness in the early 1930s. The lake had plenty of strange lore to choose from when it came to culprits for the villagers' disappearance. For instance, Angikuni has its own variation of the "Water Babies" legends from further down south. (We covered the Grey-like "Water Babies" of Pyramid Lake, Nevada, in our book *Old West UFOs.*) The water dwelling demons of Angikuni Lake were said to be scaly shapeshifters, not unlike Reptilian aliens in that regard.

Victorian Era Engraving of Innuit Village.

Regardless of what had taken the villagers, Labelle had no desire to stay in the village overnight, no matter how badly he needed shelter, and fled. Upon arrival at a telegraph office many miles away, Labelle reported his find to the Royal Canadian Mounted Police in Churchill. Eventually, Labelle and the Mounties took off together and found the village just as Labelle had left it. More disturbing yet, they discovered that some of the village graves had also been opened, and the bodies exhumed without a trace as well! [Conflicting reports state that all the graves were opened, while others say it was only one.] One hundred yards from the village, frozen dog carcasses were also found. If the tribe had fled, they most certainly would have taken their dogs with them, another mystery piece of the puzzle. And for one final, strange detail, the Mounties were said to observe pulsating, bluish lights on the horizon of the village.

Postcard of Royal Mounted Canadian Police.

The key word there was the Mounties were "said" to observe the lights. As it stands, the story has been added to quite a bit over the years since the story was first published in *Le Pas, Manitoba* on November 28, 1930. In fact, for a time, it was thought that the article didn't exist at all. Before the days of swift, online searches on sites like newspaperarchive.com, people had to rely on things like microfiche or books that reprinted old articles. One such book was Frank Edwards' *Stranger than Science*, published in 1959. Since that was the only source anyone could find for the story for many years, rumors began that Edwards' was making the article up! But, as you can see from screengrabs within this chapter, the article was indeed real. This wasn't confirmed until the 2000s, however, meaning that for nearly forty years between the 1960s to the 2000s the story's credibility was severely damaged.

It was *Fate Magazine* that reignited interest in the story nearly 20 years after Edwards' book. In fact, the article on the Angikuni disappearance was that issue's cover story, written by Dwight Whalen, for the November 1976 issue. Whalen did manage to get the RCMP to admit to investigating the case and finding an abandoned village, though in their opinion it was nothing unusual. It was simply a case of an abandoned village, be it seasonally or permanently and nothing to be concerned about. At least, that was the official story.

The first person to point to an alien explanation for the disappearance was none other than Betty Hill herself. The former abductee read Whalen's article in *Fate* and wrote a letter which was published in the April 1977 issue of *Fate*. In it, Betty explained that she and Barney, her equally famous abductee husband, had met a Captain Larsen of the Mounted Police while on a ferry ride in the Bay of Fundy. Apparently they got to talking about UFOs, and Larsen explained to the Hills his fascination with the Angikuni Lake case. After nine years of research, it was his opinion that the disappearance was the result of a mass abduction.

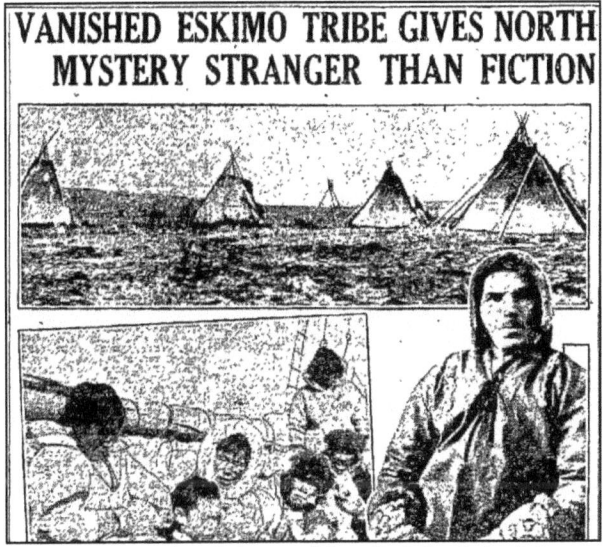

Screengrab of One of the Original Articles

In the 1980s, new layers were added to the story—keyword added. The 1983 book *The World's Great UFO Mysteries* by Nigel Blundell and Roger Boar changed many key details of the story in odd ways, bumping the village population from a mere thirty people to over a thousand! Their version of the tale was the same as the earlier ones, but what they added was an additional detail whereas the investigation of the RCMP was concerned. When the RCMP went to investigate in January of 1931, they allegedly ran across three trappers comprised of a man, Armand Laurent, and his two sons. They claimed to see strange lights moving in the air and flying toward Angikuni Lake. Not only that, these "lights" could change shape. Initially, they said the object looked like a cylinder but transformed into something more akin to a bullet as it flew towards Angikuni Lake.

Again, it's unknown just where the authors got this startling new information. As the story picked up more and more interest, the RCMP did their best to discount it with the following statement:

The story about the disappearance in the 1930's of an Inuit village near Lake Angikuni is not true. An American author by the name of Frank Edwards is purported to have started this story in his book *Stranger than Science*. It has become a popular piece of journalism, repeatedly published and referred to in books and magazines. There is no evidence however to support such a story. A village with such a large population would not have existed in such a remote area of the Northwest Territories (62 degrees north and 100 degrees west, about 100 km west of Eskimo Point). Furthermore, the Mounted Police who patrolled the area recorded no untoward events of any kind and neither did local trappers or missionaries.

The first thing that RCMP gets wrong in their statement is the claim that the story originated in *Stranger than Science*, which, again, was published in the late 1950s. The story did for a fact originate in a late November 1930 article that was circulated in many different papers. The other lie was that the

RCMP didn't investigate the incident, when they actually did. Was this an example of an early government cover-up of a strange event potentially related to UFOs?

As stated before, prior to the present day, many people claimed that the original 1930 article never existed to begin with, which, for many years, appeared to hammer a nail into the story's coffin. Today, we know that the article does exist, but that doesn't legitimize the story and there are more than a few problems with it. Chiefly, the article sports a copyright, which is unusual for non-fiction articles as opposed to fictional stories. It has been suggested that the writer, Emmett E. Kelleher, did so because he didn't want his story copied verbatim without his name on it, but it's still unusual.

Unfortunately, we can leave you with no solid conclusion to this mystery only other than to say it is certainly one of the greatest "cold cases" in all of ufology!

Woman Says Strange Object Flew by Her Bed in Yard

BY JANICE WILLIAMS.

Have you sighted saucers or disks or other strange objects in the sky lately?

Think nothing of it—you're not the first to see them. Mrs. Cleo Gaynor of 1628 E. Hattie first saw such an airborne object 11 years ago, and she says it has been on her mind ever since.

What's more, she could have reached out and touched it if she had wanted to. Instead, she just lay still and stared at the strange visitation hovering by her bed in the back yard.

Suddenly Disappeared.

Surrounding it was a blue-green glow, very soft, Mrs. Gaynor, still on her elbow, watched as the craft moved toward the foot of her bed, then suddenly zoomed into the sky and disappeared.

When she called her mother and a friend, they told her she had been dreaming, but she knows that she was wide awake and the craft was no dream. She's thought about it often ever since, but hasn't talked much about it. It's a matter of pride.

Portion of Article from Fort Worth (Tx.) Star-Telegram, 3-24-1950, p. 23.

UNEARTHLY DRONE

Fort Worth, Texas
August or September 1939

IN OUR PREVIOUS BOOKS in this series, we have included several stories, from as far back as the 1800s, about people who encountered mysterious, high-tech flying objects that resembled modern drones. Considering that consumer-grade drones were not available until 2006, where did such advanced technology come from in these early sightings of drones? Could they have been surveillance devices unleashed upon the planet by extraterrestrials?

Thus, we come to an interesting sighting in 1939 of a small object that the eyewitness referred to as a "flying saucer," but which was obviously very small in terms of conventional UFOs. The object was approximately three feet long and about one foot high, according to the witness, which almost exactly fits the dimensions of a modern drone.

A Modern Drone (PixShere.com)

The sighting occurred in either August or September of 1939 near 1700 East Tucker Street in Fort Worth, Texas -- in the backyard of the childhood residence of the eyewitness, Ms. Cleo Gayner. She kept the story of the encounter to herself until 1950, when she told it to reporter Janice Williams of the *Fort Worth Star-Telegram,* who published it on March 24, 1950. Gaynor was no doubt encouraged to report her incident by the thousands of UFO reports that were filed by Americans from 1947 to 1950.

The encounter began late on a moonlit night while she was sleeping on a bed in the backyard of her parents' home. She was startled awake by a loud whirring noise "like an electric fan" coming from the east. Raising herself up on an elbow, she looked around for the source of the noise. What she saw frightened her so greatly that she felt the incident affected her for the remainder of her life.

Mississippi Steamboat Natchez (Public Domain)

A short distance from her, hovering about 20 or 30 feet in the air was a metallic gray flying object that seemed to have "veins" running through its surface. A soft blue-green glow surrounded the object as it slowly maneuvered closer to where Gaynor lay in bed. The closest thing she could find to compare it to was "an old-time Mississippi steamboat with a deck around the bottom."

Gaynor, still propped up on an elbow, remained perfectly still, barely venturing to breathe, as the strange apparition descended to a height even with the mattress on her bed, where it just "hovered in midair." It was close enough for her to have reached out and touched it, she later told the newspaper report. Moments after it descended to hover at the food of her bed, the strange object suddenly zoomed into the sky and disappeared.

Gaynor told her mother and a friend but was met with resistance to her story. They said that she must have dreamed the whole episode, but she insisted that she had been wide awake during the encounter and that the strange craft was no dream.

The *Fort Worth Star-Telegram* article concluded with, "She's thought about it often ever since but hasn't talked much about it. It's a matter of pride. Since saucer sighting flared anew, she's been watching the skies at night .... She's going to keep on watching hoping she will get a chance again to see the mysterious object that visited her before the day of saucers."

FLAMING AIRSHIP
CRASH IN
MOTHMAN COUNTRY

Point Pleasant, West Virginia
October 11, 1931

IF THIS 1931 FLAMING CRASH of a 100-foot-long diameter airship near Point Pleasant, West Virginia, is true, it might have marked the arrival on Earth of the so-called "Mothman," an unearthly winged humanoid that terrorized Point Pleasant in the 1960s, leading to the writing of a book, John Keel's *The Mothman Prophecies* (1975), and at least two movies.

Since the first reported appearance of the Mothman in Point Pleasant was in 1966, perhaps the creature took 35 years to mature fully after landing upon the Earth in an immature form, back in 1931? In any event, whether it is connected to the Mothman or not, the UFO crash itself presents us with a very interesting story, which we shall examine next.

Artist's Depiction of Mothman
by Tim Bertelink - Own work, CC BY-SA 4.0,
https://commons.wikimedia.org/w/index.php?curid=46584699

On the evening of Saturday, October 10, 1931, witnesses observed the fiery crash of a 100-foot-long airship in the hills just south of Point Pleasant. Newspaper accounts said, "Some persons who witnessed the accident described the blimp as plunging to the ground in flames, men leaping from it in parachutes as it fell." Another group of witnesses told the newspaper of "seeing the craft fly over and then burst into flames and fall."

BLIMP IS BELIEVED DOWN IN WOODED SECTION OF STATE

Searching Party Is Organized At Point Pleasant To Comb Hills

GALLIPOLIS PLANES WILL START SEARCH AT DAWN

Half Dozen Cities Report Seeing Dirigible Break In Two And Fall In Flames; Believe Craft En Route To Huntington; Goodyear Ships Safe

Point Pleasant, W. Va., October 10. (AP)—A searching party organized by Point Pleasant police tonight started toward the hills back of Gallipolis Ferry, behind which a blimp was reported to have fallen in flames.

The party was organized after Robert P. Henke, of Gallipolis, his wife and Dr. and Mrs. Claude Carter, also of Gallipolis, said they saw the blimp cross the Ohio river and that it fell while Henke was watching it through field glasses. Henke, building contractor, said the blimp was between 100 and 150 feet long and flying at an altitude of about 300 feet when it burst. He said that a moment before it fell behind hills back of Gallipolis Ferry he saw something white, which may have been a parachute, floating downward.

Bluefield (VA.) Daily Telegraph, 10-11-1931, p.1.

Shortly after midnight, Sheriff H. E. Burdette, state trooper H. E. Pomroy, and a number of other men, initiated a search in the densely wooded area, looking for evidence of a crash or survivors. Joining in the search were volunteers from nearby Gallipolis, Ohio, located directly on the other side of the Ohio River from Point Pleasant. After scouring the woods for hours and finding not a trace, the party returned to their homes at dawn. Other parties continued the search during the day on Sunday, October 11, while authorities asked local airports and airfields if they had any missing aircraft. None were reported.

In the meantime, Lieutenant Eckford Hodson took off from the Gallipolis airport and made three separate flights throughout the day on Sunday without spotting a trace of wreckage or survivors. Also, known airship companies were contacted, but all of them said they had no ships aloft in West Virginia.

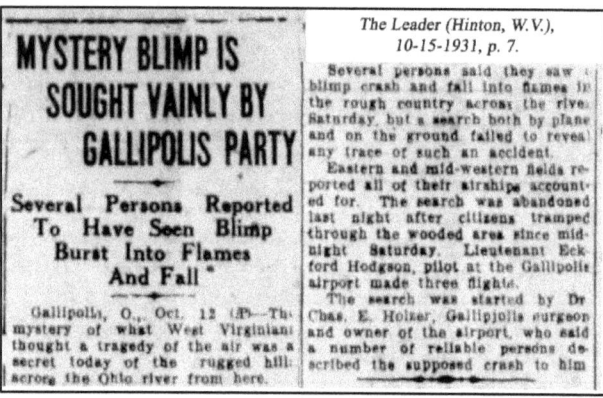

The Leader (Hinton, W.V.),
10-15-1931, p. 7.

MYSTERY BLIMP IS SOUGHT VAINLY BY GALLIPOLIS PARTY

Several Persons Reported
To Have Seen Blimp
Burst Into Flames
And Fall

Gallipolis, O., Oct. 12 (AP)—The mystery of what West Virginians thought a tragedy of the air was a secret today of the rugged hills across the Ohio river from here.

Several persons said they saw a blimp crash and fall into flames in the rough country across the river Saturday, but a search both by plane and on the ground failed to reveal any trace of such an accident.

Eastern and mid-western fields reported all of their airships accounted for. The search was abandoned last night after citizens tramped through the wooded area since midnight Saturday. Lieutenant Eckford Hodgson, pilot at the Gallipolis airport made three flights.

The search was started by Dr. Chas. E. Holzer, Gallipolis surgeon and owner of the airport, who said a number of reliable persons described the supposed crash to him.

After the search for the fallen craft continued all day on Sunday, it was concluded that there was nothing to be found. The strange object, which was totally unaccounted for, had apparently vanished in thin air. Despite the testimony of the witnesses that a dramatic, fiery crash had taken place in the hills, nothing was ever found, and no missing aircraft were ever reported to have been flying in the area.

Local newspapers reported, "Search for a blimp reported to have crashed and burned in the hills south of this city was abandoned tonight after a fruitless all-day quest by parties afoot and in the air. [Searchers] said they would lead no more searching parties and Lieutenant Eckford Hodgson, pilot at the Gallipolis, Ohio, airport, after three flights seeking the blimp, said he would not go aloft again."

The *Wilkes-Barre (Penn.) Record* reported, "Hodgson made an airplane flight shortly after dawn over the wooded areas for an hour and a half. He went up again about noon and again just before darkness and rain made flying impossible .... Hodgson has made several flights over the vicinity where the crash was reported, but said

Huge Bird-Like Creature Seen In State

Mason County Monster

PT. PLEASANT — Would you believe a seven-foot tall bird-like creature with large red eyes and a cruising speed of 100 miles an hour?

There are four young people in this Ohio River community who say they saw it and they are willing to take a lie detector test to satisfy disbelievers.

It all started shortly before midnight Wednesday when Steve Mallette, 20, and his wife of five months, Mary, and another young married couple, Roger and Linda Scarberry, were joyriding five miles from here.

"We came over a little rise in the road out near the old power plant when we saw the eyes over in the bushes. They glowed red and were six inches apart," Mallette said.

They all saw it...the eyes glowing weirdly in the bush. Mallette, a hunter since he was six, brushed it off as a coon or another animal.

They then steered their car out of the 2,500-acre maze of dirt roads and fish ponds which make up the McClintic Wildlife Station. It's located in what's known as the TNT area, an abandoned U.S. Ordnance com-

plex.

"When we reached the paved road there it was again sitting on the bank across the road," Mallette continued.

The second sighting revealed the creature's man-like form, they said. It stood over six feet tall, its wings protruding from the center of its back "like an angel."

Its torso resembled a human except it had no arms and the face was hard to distinguish. It walked clumsy, "like a penguin," and when it raised its wings to a 10-foot span it "went straight up."

By this time the two women were crying. Scarberry didn't waste any time heading for the city.

"I'm not one to scare easy," he said, "but I was for getting out of there."

On the trip back to Pt. Pleasant at speeds between 100 and 105 mph, the "thing" hovered above the car, casting a dark shadow over the rear window.

"I was doing 100-105 mph and it was just gliding over top, sorta moving from side to side. Then it came down at the car, making a squealing noise like a mouse," Scarberry said.

The Raleigh Register (Beckley, W.V.), 11-17-1966, p. 2.

he saw nothing that would aid in clearing up the mystery surrounding the supposed crash."

The strange incident was bizarre enough to be mentioned in the *New York Times* in an article on October 11, 1931, reporting the claims that a flaming 100-foot blimp swooped low (300 feet) over the Ohio River, but all the dirigible companies denied any of their craft were missing or even flying in the West Virginia region.

Thirty-five years later, a very strange humanoid creature began stalking the woods near where the airship reportedly crashed. The very first reported sighting of the humanoid appeared on November 16, 1966, in the *Point Pleasant Register* newspaper with the headline "Couples See Man-Sized Bird...Creature...Something." The full text of the article follows:

"It was a bird... or something. It definitely wasn't a flying saucer."

Two Point Pleasant couples said today they encountered a man-sized, bird-like creature in the TNT area about midnight last night.

Sheriff's deputies and City Police went to the scene about 2 o'clock this morning but were unable to spot anything.

But the two young men telling their story this morning were dead serious and asserted they hadn't been drinking.

Steve Mallette of 3305 Jackson Avenue and Roger Scarberry of 809 30th Street described the thing as being about six or seven feet tall, having a wingspan of 10 feet and red eyes about two inches in diameter and six inches apart.

"It was like a man with wings," Mallette said. "It wasn't like anything you'd see on TV or in a monster movie..."

The men and their wives were in Scarberry's car between 11:30 p.m. and midnight when they spotted the creature near the old power plant adjacent to the old National Guard Armory buildings.

The creature was seen standing on three occasions and was described as being extremely fast ("it flew about 100 miles an hour") in flight but was a clumsy (sic) runner.

Deputy Millard Halstead said he had seen dust in the vicinity of a coal field. But "it could have been" caused by the bird, he said.

"I'm a hard guy to scare" Scarberry said, "but last night I was for getting out of there."

They did just that, but the "thing" followed them. They said it was hovering over the car, apparently gliding, until they reached the National Guard Armory on Route 62.

"We went downtown, turned around, and went back and there it was again," Mallette said. "It seemed to be waiting on us." He said the light-grey-like creature then scurried through a field. It also had flown across the top of the car.

"It apparently is afraid of light," Mallette reasoned, "and maybe it thought it was scaring us off."

The young men said they saw the creature's eyes, which glowed red, only when their lights shined on it. And it seemed to want to get away from the lights.

They said it looked like a "man with wings" but that the head was "not an outstanding characteristic."

Both were slightly pale and tired from lack of sleep during the night following their harrowing experience.

They speculated that the thing was living in the vacant power plant, possibly in one of the huge boilers. "There are pigeons in all the other buildings," Mallette said, "but not in that one."

"If I had seen it while by myself I wouldn't have said anything," Scarberry commented, "but there were four of us who saw it."

They said it didn't resemble a bat in any way, but "maybe what you would visualize as an angel."

The last time they saw it was at the gate of the C. C. Lewis farm on Route 62.

They heard a sound like wings flapping and they said the bird rose straight up, like a helicopter.

"This doesn't have an explanation to it," Mallette said, "It was an animal but nothing like I've seen before."

Are they going back to look for the creature?

"Yes," Mallette said, "this afternoon and again tonight."

"Today," Scarberry said, "but tonight, I don't know."

Perhaps there is no real connection between the Mothman and the mysterious 1931 crash of an unidentified airship in the hills outside Point Pleasant, West Virginia. Then again, maybe there is? We may never know for sure, although it seems awfully coincidental that these two eerie events would both happen within a radius of just a few miles, although separated in time by 35 years.

UFO HUMANOID ENCOUNTER

Greensboro, North Carolina
May 1930

A VERY INTERESTING UFO encounter happened in May of 1930 to sisters Katherine Rankin and Mary Rankin at their childhood home on Pearson Street in Greensboro, North Carolina. The incident was witnessed by the two of them and by their parents, Mr. and Mrs. J. T. Rankin. The case was kept "hidden" within the family until after the parents had both passed away, after which it was disclosed by the Rankin sisters.

The incident began on a clear, bright day when a dark-colored UFO shaped like a toy spinning top and about 40 feet wide approached the Rankin residence on Pearson Street in Greensboro, hovering over their backyard.

Old Fashioned Spinning Top
(Image by Alberto Adán from Pixabay)

The family of four watched in amazement as the object made a soft landing in their backyard. As they continued observing, they noticed that the landed craft had a "window," through which they could see that the interior was "hollow."

But the most amazing part of their encounter was yet to unfold. As they peered at the window in the craft, they were startled to see a humanoid suddenly appear inside the ship. Although they could only see the figure's head and shoulders, they could tell he was wearing a helmet on his head and also a dark, tight-fitting uniform.

Spacesuit Exhibit (NASA)

The family continued watching in stunned silence for about five or ten minutes as the mysterious figure moved around inside the craft, after which they observed that the craft appeared to be lifting off.

The object began ascending straight up into the air, making virtually no sound. It then zoomed away, exhibiting the ability to move both vertically and horizontally, according to the witnesses.

The Rankin sisters finally broke their silence in 1975, telling their unusual tale to a leading UFO researcher named George D. Fawcett (1929 - 2013), who was a long time UFO advocate in North Carolina, author, lecturer, and founder of the North Carolina chapter of the Mutual UFO Network (MUFON).

GEORGE D. FAWCETT

The Greenville (S.C.) News, 8-22-1973, p. 27.

After revealing their story to Fawcett in 1975, the Rankin sisters subsequently gave a series of interviews about their family's strange UFO encounter. It is certainly one of the strangest of the reported UFO events from the 1930s.

SHRIEKING BIGFOOT SIGHTING

Mineola, New York
June 29, 1931

PIONEERING PARANORMAL researcher Charles Fort was drawn to a strange tale of an ape-like humanoid creature that was seen in Mineola, Long Island, New York, on June 29, 1931. In the final book before his death, titled *Wild Talents* (1932), Fort included this brief mention: "New York Times, June 30, 1931 – 'Police at Mineola hunt ape-like animal -- hairy creature, about four feet tall.'" The monstrous apparition "is said to have a hairy chest and big feet and is believed to be a large monkey, a chimpanzee, an ape -- *or something else.*"

Charles Fort, Pioneer of Paranormal Research

Although the newspaper accounts stated that the creature might have escaped from a circus, no escaped beast was reported by any circus or zoo. Said the newspapers, "A hairy jungle denizen, believed to be an ape, which threw mothers in a panic in the neighborhood of Albertson Square, on the outskirts of Mineola late yesterday, was the object of a hunt by posses armed with shotguns and tear gas bombs in nearby dense woods."

According to newspaper accounts, the beast had been glimpsed on at least a dozen occasions over the course of 10 days near Albertson Square and East Williston. Witnesses saw the creature "swinging in trees" along the edges of the nearby forest. Among those who saw the beast was the wife of Police Sergeant Berkeley Hyde, who saw it in the front yard of her residence.

Some of the witnesses stated that the beast was about four feet tall, while others put its height at closer to six feet. Until June 29, there had been no close-up encounters involving the ape-like being. Judging by witness accounts, the creature seems to have been analogous to "Bigfoot," also known as Sasquatch.

On the 29th, a 7-year-old boy, George Ballis, was playing alone on the baseball field at Albertson Square when the strange beast left the cover of the nearby woods, jumped up on the wire backstop of the baseball diamond and, swinging its long arms, began climbing nimbly.

Suddenly spotting the boy down below, the hairy beast dropped to the ground and uttered an ear-splitting "horrible shriek." It then approached to within 10 feet of the boy, who was rooted to the spot in fright.

A passing man noticed what was happening, and he yelled to the boy to run away and go home. At the same time, the man picked up a stone and threw it, striking the animal in the chest. The creature responded by emitting another terrifying shriek and then fled back into the woods.

Local police, upon learning of the apparent attempted attack on the boy, immediately started a hunt in the woods for the beast. They were joined by heavily armed men forming a posse to conduct the search. Altogether, a dozen police officers and 40 citizens began beating through the woods.

Strange Beast Is Seen, Posses Take Its Trail

Animal, Believed to Be Ape Escaped from Circus, Frightens Mothers Near Mineola—Approached Boy at Play.

Special to the Pittsburgh Post-Gazette and the Chicago Tribune.

MINEOLA, L. I., June 30. — A hairy jungle denizen, believed to be an ape, which threw mothers in a panic in the neighborhood of Albertson Square, on the outskirts of Mineola late yesterday, was the object of a hunt by posses armed with shotguns and tear gas bombs in nearby dense woods.

A dozen patrolmen of the Nassau county police, flanked by two score citizens, began beating through the woods after the creature had frightened a seven-year-old boy at play with "a horrible shriek."

The beast, described variously as being from four and a half to six feet tall, has been reported seen a dozen times in the last 10 days in Albertson Square and East Williston.

Only fleeting glimpses of the animal, swinging in trees on the outskirts of the woodland, were reported until it invaded a baseball diamond in Albertson Square. George Ballis, 7, was playing alone, when he saw the beast climbing nimbly up the wire backstop. Swinging its long arms, the hairy creature, believed to have escaped from a circus, dropped to the ground upon seeing the boy, and approached within 10 feet of him. Little George stood rooted to the spot.

A man, who later boarded a bus after telling the boy to run home, hit the animal in the chest with a stone. Emitting a terrifying shriek the creature turned and fled to the woods.

Police Captain Earle Comstock started a hunt immediately he was notified. He had received four other complaints.

Pittsburgh (PA.) Post-Gazette, 7-1-1931, p. 26.

Although the creature was never found, the searchers did discover the tracks of "big, bare feet" in the soft dirt of an open field in Mineola. One police officer told reporters that he "planned to spread bananas and salt, with traps, if the beast was not captured."

After not being able to locate the beast, some of the searchers wondered if the whole episode had been a "spoof" (i.e., hoax); however, the problem with the hoax theory is that so many different people (at least 12) reported seeing the creature over so many days (at least 10).

POLICE END HUNT FOR MINEOLA "APE"

Animal Said to Have Been Seen by Several Persons.

Mineola, June 30.—Police of Mineola today determined to quit searching for the animal reported to be at large here and which is said to have a hairy chest and big feet and is believed to be a large monkey, a chimpanzee, an ape—or something else.

The wife of Police Sergeant Berkeley Hyde, of Williston Park, said she saw the animal on her front lawn. Some boys claimed the animal was trying to climb the high backstop on a baseball field here, and several people have reported seeing prints of "big, bare feet," in the soft earth of an open field in the village. Sergeant Hyde and four assistants, armed with shotguns, searched for the animal yesterday and when they found no trace of it, quit in disgust, somewhat more than half-convinced that somebody was spoofing them.

If it is an ape, it was said, it might have escaped from one of several circuses which have visited this section recently.

Times Union (Brooklyn, NY), 6-30-1931, p. 9.

Depiction of Bigfoot by Artist Neil Reibe

Might this have actually been a sighting of the so-called Bigfoot, also known as Sasquatch? The witness descriptions seem to match those of Bigfoot, namely that of a hairy humanoid with big feet. In most Bigfoot sightings, the creature is described as between 6 and 9 feet tall – so this 1931 sighting is generally in the range (4 to 6 feet). The location of the sighting, New York, is actually number 5 among U.S. states with the most Bigfoot sightings, trailing only Washington state, California, Pennsylvania, and Michigan. So, a genuine Sasquatch sighting in New York in 1931? Possibly! And, to harken back to Fort's comments that it could be "a large monkey, a chimpanzee, an ape – *or something else...*" Maybe even something from beyond the stars?

ALIENS AT THE U.S. CAPITOL

Washington, D.C.
Circa 1935

THE STORY OF A RECOVERED UFO and alien bodies preserved in large glass jars in a secret chamber under the U.S. Capitol Building in 1935 sounds like the plot of a science-fiction novel. And yet, many believe this story to be the absolute truth, mostly due to the source – the daughters of Reverend Turner Hamilton Holt, a cousin of U.S. Secretary of State Cordell Hull, who served in office under President Franklin D. Roosevelt from 1933 to 1945.

According to Lucile and Allene Holt, they were each told independently by their father that Cordell Hull personally showed Reverend Holt a wrecked circular craft of some kind and four large glass jars holding creatures that looked somewhat human but were not. These artifacts were stored in a sub-basement of the U.S. Capitol building in Washington, D.C.

The sisters were told this story in 1948, when Holt was serving as minister at the Shenandoah Christian Church in Greenwich, Ohio, in the 1940s. Holt was born in 1894 and died in 1960.

U.S. Capitol Building
By Martin Falbisoner - Own work, CC BY-SA 3.0, Wikipedia

Prior to being shown the amazing artifacts, Reverend Holt agreed never to reveal the secret. His daughters, Lucile and Allene, heard the secret from their father but resolved to never reveal it to anyone until well after his death. It wasn't until 2000, 65 years after Holt was shown the alien craft and bodies, that the sisters wrote an incredible letter to the Ohio chapter of the Mutual UFO Network [MUFON] disclosing their father's experience.

The letter said:

Today I want to share some knowledge that has been, by request, kept secret in our family since sometime in World War II. This concerns something my father was shown by his cousin Cordell Hull, the Secretary of State under Franklin Roosevelt. Sumner Wells was his Under-Secretary of State. Hull was a cousin to my father. My father was on some kind of advising committee, and made several trips to Washington, D.C., in that capacity.

My father, who was young, brilliant, and sound of mind tells this story to us because he didn't want the information to be lost. One day when my father was in D.C., with Cordell, Cordell swore him to secrecy and took him to a sub-basement in the U.S. Capitol building and showed him an amazing sight: (1) Four large glass jars holding 4 creatures unknown to my father or Cordell, (2) A wrecked round craft of some kind nearby.

My father wanted my sister and I to make this information known long after he and Cordell were dead, because he felt it was a very important bit of information. We have researched your group [MUFON] and feel it is the most reliable group in the country. We hope that you will research and search this information.

Please don't disregard this, because what I have written is true. The jars with creatures in formaldehyde and the wrecked craft are somewhere!

Cordell said they were afraid they would start a panic if the public found out about it.

Sincerely, Lucille Andrew - Ashland, Ohio

*Tennessee Senator Cordell Hull Served as U.S.
Secretary of State from 1933 to 1944
(Library of Congress)*

The letter was definitely an eye-opener, and much research was done by MUFON and other groups on the story told by Lucile and Allene. The following points were soon confirmed:

- Reverend Holt and Secretary Hull grew up in the same area of Kentucky, knew each other quite well, and were apparently distant cousins.

- The U.S. Capitol building in 1931 did have a sub-basement that was divided into smaller "storage rooms."

Although Hull left extensive papers from his years as Secretary of State, no reference has ever been found in these documents regarding the secrets hidden below the U.S. Capitol in 1931. However, since he swore Reverend Hull to secrecy before disclosing the matter to him, it seems reasonable that he would not have revealed anything in his memoirs or papers.

Finally, history shows that Revered Holt was considered a very honest and trustworthy member of the clergy, he seems a reliable source of information for this story.

Both Lucile and Allene Holt passed away in 2009, nine years after disclosing their father's incredible story. They accomplished the mission given to them by Reverend Holt – to not allow the story about what he saw in the Capitol Sub-Basement to be forgotten.

Shortly before their passing, the sisters gave a video interview to MUFON investigators, in which they carefully retold the story of their dad's experience, which we will recount below, using their actual words.

*Cordell Hull Leaving the White House on 11-9-
1935 (Library of Congress)*

Allene started the interview by saying, "My father
was the Reverend Turner Holt, and he came to
visit me one day in around about 1948. I know that
because that was when my oldest daughter was a
toddler, and we were watching her play and we
were talking."

She said her father told her, "You know, there's
something I want to tell you. I think someone in
my family should know about this besides me."

The reverend explained to Allene that his cousin,
Cordell Hull, had sworn him to secrecy about the
incident, but Holt felt at the time "that I should tell
you so that someone in the family would know."

Reverend Holt then launched into a description of what happened back in 1935 in Washington, D.C. "He told me about going to Washington for a conference, I think it was called, of ministers of all denominations from all over the country. And he was a representative from this area, and why he was chosen as probably because Cordell Hull put his name in the box because it wouldn't be very likely that anyone in Washington would have picked a preacher from a little town like Shenandoah."

Allene continued her amazing narrative: "And so while he was there, I am not sure how they got together, but he and his cousin, Cordell Hull, I think it was third or fourth cousin ... something like that. And he got together with him at the State Capitol building. That's where Cordell wanted him to be. I don't know if they went to lunch first or if they just met there, and Cordell said that he wanted to show him something. And he said, "But you have to swear that you'll never, ever tell anybody". And so he did. And so they started down, down in the building."

According to Allene, as they descended to the lower depths of the Capitol, the reverend turned to Hull and asked where they were going, to which Hull only replied, "Well, you'll see." And they continued down past the regular basement to a sub-basement below it.

In the sub-basement, they walked along a long hallway that was lighted, but the rooms off to the sides of the passage were dark. Finally arriving at one specific room, Cordell Hull opened the door, reached in to turn on the light switch, and said, "Now this is something really strange that is down here."

Inside the lighted room, Reverend Holt was shocked to see three or four large glass jars that were on top of "some kind of stand." Floating inside the jars in what Holt assumed was formaldehyde were the bodies of "little people."

Holt later told his daughters, "They were like people, but they weren't. They had all the same things that we have, but it seemed to me like their heads were a little too large for their body. I think their eyes were bigger than ours."

As far as the height of the bodies, Holt had difficulty remembering exactly. He was sure they were shorter than adult humans, and after being pressed on the issue by Allene, Holt finally settled on a height of about four feet.

After Hull showed him the bodies, he led Holt into an adjacent area that contained "some kind of a machine." Allene remembered, "That, he said, was a flying machine of some sort." The object was saucer shaped and had sustained significant damage. "Yeah, it was in pieces, all wrecked," Allene said. "Dad said it was really, really pretty shiny, but he said it wasn't anything that he'd ever seen before - so he couldn't say what kind of material it was."

Astonishingly, Hull went over to the saucer and instructed Holt to try picking up a piece of the wreckage. When the reverend did so, he found that the piece was extremely lightweight."

"As far as I know, they didn't explain anything to him," Allene said, "They just wanted him to see it, and then they left."

Lucille was told the story separately by her father, although she did not remember exactly when. She said, "I don't remember. It was when I was young. He thought somebody eventually should know about this, about the creatures he saw. Now I remember his saying [something about] three glass jars with... and he referred to them as creatures in them. He didn't say people or animals, he said creatures that he had never seen before."

Both sisters said the incident was never mentioned again for the rest of Holt's life. Lucille said "I think he sort of had it a guilty conscience that he had promised [Hull] not to tell. But as time went on, he realized that somebody should know about this, you know?"

1940 U.S. Census Showing the Turner Holt Houshold

As far as what year Holt was shown the artifacts, Allene believes it was 1935. "He didn't mention the year, but it was when Cordell [Hull] was secretary of state under Roosevelt and the letters I have are dated 1935, and that was when he was in Washington."

Asked why she wrote the letter to MUFON in 2000, Lucille said, "So I felt somebody should know about this. This is as I grew older and maybe hopefully got a little more sense in my head. I thought, this is something that is very important and hearing about the Roswell thing and, and other things. I thought this galaxy we live in the Milky Way is huge and there has to be a lot of life in it. This was my thought and I thought for that reason, someone should know about this."

Lucille added that her son, a Harvard graduate and scientist, tried to persuade her not to reveal the story. "He didn't want us to tell it because he thought we could get into a really jumbled mess. But we were telling the truth and the truth always. It doesn't get you in trouble unless you've committed a crime, you know?"

Apparently, the reported crash of a UFO near Roswell, New Mexico, in July 1947, was a main motivation for her to reveal the story. She said, "I just felt this must be told as because the Roswell thing. Made me think something is going on."

Lucille also stated a very interesting theory about why her dad and hundreds of other ministers from throughout the United States were called to Washington, D.C. in 1935. "I think the reason dad was appointed to this committee in Washington is called world order. And the thing was that they were afraid that we would be invaded by a lot of these so-called creatures, and that goodness only knows what would happen. And Dad's job around in this area was to calm people down and help people cope and find other people who could help other ministers and whoever could help cope with an invasion from outer space or from one of these other solar systems."

Allene (left) and Lucille (right) During MUFON Video Interview in 2000

When asked how people reacted to their revelation of their dad's story, Lucille said, "Well, very guarded reaction from people, which is understandable. Most people don't believe it. You know, and that's understandable. And but if you're a scientist or scientific minded, you realize that there can be there has to be a lot of life out there of one kind or another. And a lot of it could be a lot smarter than we are. Most of it probably is. You know, and that's my thought that this ought to be general knowledge because we might have to, who knows, we might have to defend ourselves."

Regardless of the skepticism, Lucille expressed her complete belief in her dad's story. "He was a very honest man, had all his faculties and very he was also a very intelligent man. Very, very intelligent anyway."

And finally, an unanswered question that is of great concern to UFO researchers – from where did the U.S. government recover the UFO and alien bodies that were allegedly stored at the Capitol? In 1931, we know of only one widely reported UFO crash in America that could have yielded crash debris and at least one body, which was the 1897 crash of an unidentified airship in Aurora, Texas. In addition to Aurora, there were a number of other rumored UFO crashes with minimal or no information ever having surfaced about them.

Another possibility is that the Capitol UFO and bodies may have been recovered from a site that was never disclosed to the public. It's possible that the object and bodies were found in a remote wilderness, after which the government slammed the lid of secrecy on the finding.

PHOTOGRAPHS OF AN ALIEN AND A UFO

Alaska/Colorado
Early 1930s

✦

ACCORDING TO UFO RESEARCHER B.J. Booth of *UFOcasebook.com*, a photograph of an alleged extraterrestrial was taken in the early 1930s in Alaska. The incident was first made public in an e-mail sent to Booth's web site on August 14, 2003 from a gentleman who asked to remain anonymous.

Said the letter:

The included picture was taken by my grandfather in the early 1930s. I scanned the image immediately after he gave it to me last week.

I wish to remain anonymous since I don't want anything to do with any research or whatever on this.

I know it looks like an alien or a Bigfoot and I know my grandfather was telling me the truth about him taking this picture. That's why I think it should be in the right hands.

You are the only one I'm sending this to, so please respect my privacy and don't contact me about this.

Thanks in advance,

[name redacted]

Photo of Alleged Alien in Alaska, circa Early 1930s

There was also a caption below the photograph, which read: "The picture was taken in the early 1930s by my grandfather, who lived in Alaska in those days. He first saw this entity when he was in his car driving towards a lake. He chased the entity up until this point where he made this picture of it. It took him four months to develop the picture since it wasn't easy back in those days to develop a picture, especially in Alaska. I got this picture last week. My grandfather died the next day."

Closer View of Alleged ET

Booth, who did extensive research into the photograph, said, "To say the least, I was intrigued by this mysterious message. What could this image be? I downloaded it, and after looking at it a few moments, I knew it would be controversial to say the least. Little did I know that there would be more than one mystery to solve."

Booth added, "As I began the task of selecting and cutting the area around the small creature, I thought to myself: 'Wouldn't it be something if this was the real thing, even though it may never be proven as such?

"What if this gentleman's grandfather had really filmed a creature from another world, and I was looking at the proof. My excitement was only tempered by the thought of not being able to prove it one way or the other. I would soon be faced, however, with the second mystery."

Upon attempting several different methods of photographic analysis, Booth thought he spotted a blurry shape near the creature's right arm. "The entity's right lower arm/hand region seemed to be obscured; but by what? So I went back to the original scan and starting working on that particular area. What I finally saw, or thought I saw, was a second, even smaller entity. Is it possible that we had a female with her child?"

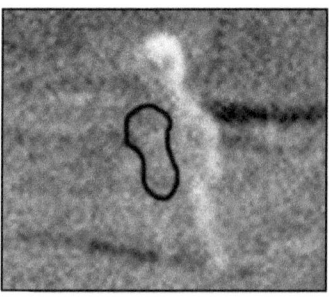

Booth felt that his analysis, while interesting, was not conclusive. The image could still be anything from an outright hoax to a genuine unexplained creature or creatures.

As one studies the photograph carefully, it is extremely difficult to identify what the creature has in its right arm, if anything. If not a "child," perhaps the creature is holding a weapon or other device.

Although there have been other purported photographs of extraterrestrials over the years, this one is among the most impressive. The photo seems to fit the stated location (Alaska) and the stated time period (1930s).

It does seem to work against credibility that the author of the e-mail refuses to be contacted or questioned further. In many cases, that tactic would raise a red flag and point to a possible hoax. Then again many people prefer not to be contacted about the UFO topic, desiring to maintain their privacy and fearing that they will become the "laughingstock" of their families or social groups.

Another troubling aspect of the e-mail is that the grandfather reportedly died "the next day" after the letter was received by his grandson. That part of the story seems very coincidental and somewhat convenient in terms of preventing anyone from trying to contact the grandfather.

Regarding the grandfather's age, the fact that he was driving a car in the 1930s would suggest he was at least around 20 years old. That would have made him around 90 years old in 2003, which sounds reasonable.

So, in the end, is this photograph real or not? We are not really able to say conclusively, but it remains an intriguing artifact that came down to us, purportedly, from the 1930s.

Another fascinating photograph comes to us from September 14, 1931, reportedly taken in Gunnison, Colorado, and it shows what clearly appears to be a metallic flying saucer.

On May 6, 2017, an amazing photograph was submitted to the Mutual UFO Network via its UFO reporting online form, along with this extremely brief but tantalizing description: "This is a picture of a photograph my great grandfather reportedly took. The photograph has been handed down to me."

Photo of a UFO Taken on 9-14-1931

If authentic, this photo represents one of the earliest clear photographs of a UFO taken during the 20th century. In a close up of the original photograph, we shall look at some interesting features.

First, the number 1 arrow is pointing to what appears to be a crossbar located above the metallic disk. This is an unusual feature. If not some type of rod or crossbar, then might it be a rotating blade, like on a helicopter?

Then another feature of the photo that begs our attention is a cylindrical "rod" that is just to the right and a bit below the disc-shaped UFO. The rod seems narrower on the left side and broader on the right. It appears the same shade of darkness as the saucer. It is unknown whether this was an actual artifact in the sky or whether it might have been a mark made on the picture after it was taken, or some type of artifact introduced by the photography. Marker number 3 of the map simply marks the "W" on Tenderfoot Mountain in Gunnison, a historic landmark about which we will discuss more later.

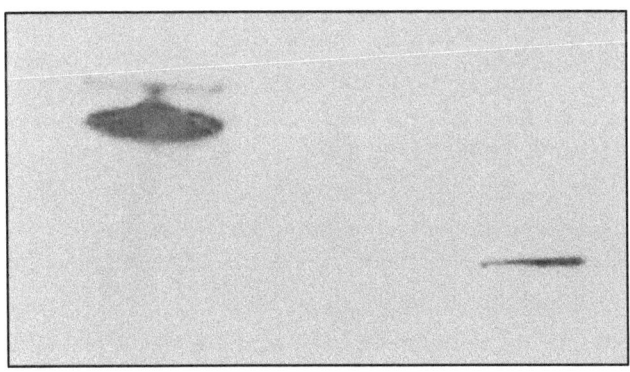

The submission of this photograph to MUFON in 2017 was quite remarkable, and it included a view of the back side of the original photograph, which is shown below:

Having a view of the back of the photo tends to lend to the feeling of authenticity. The date of September 14, 1931, is stamped on the original print, along with a print number (#26), and the processor's name, "Sunshine Quality Developing & Printing," with the slogan "Never Fade."

Of course, skeptics would argue that someone could have taken a photo of Tenderfoot Mountain back in 1931 and then digitally added a UFO to it. Or that the object appearing to be a saucer could be much closer to the camera lens than it seems to be.

Speaking of Tenderfoot Mountain, the "W" on it was constructed in 1923 by students of what was then known as Western University and is now known as Western Colorado University. According to the university's web site, "For the

6,000-plus residents of Gunnison and the many tourists and truckers alike who travel to or through the small Colorado city along U.S. Highway 50, Tenderfoot Mountain is best known for the big 'W' marked on it facing town. Many Gunnisonians know it only as W Mountain. In 1923, the same year Gunnison's Colorado State Normal School was transformed to a four-year liberal arts college known as Western, students constructed a big 'W' on the large mountain just south of campus. With rocks extending 450 feet up and down, it's America's largest college logo. And once a year, the W is set ablaze in the evening to usher in Homecoming weekend on campus."

Kodak Box Camera, Typical of the 1930s

The location is certainly correct. The construction of the houses in the photo appear to fit the period (1931). Other photos of Gunnison in the 1930s seem to fit the same general appearance.

The problem with submitting a historical photograph to an investigative group like MUFON is that, while it makes for an interesting anecdote, verification of its authenticity is virtually impossible. The photographer is not known and is almost certainly no longer living. There are no known witnesses to the sighting and no historical documents that refer to the sighting. In short, research into a photograph such as this is essentially a dead end, from the perspective of a UFO investigation. Were we to find even one document from this time (1931) referring to a strange object seen over the skies of Gunnison, then we would have a basis to possibly look at this evidence more seriously.

15
HORSEBACK UFO ENCOUNTER

Holyoake, Colorado
February 15, 1931

ON JUNE 7, 2004, the National UFO Reporting Center (NUFORC) received an online report from a 90-year-old Colorado resident who disclosed a UFO incident that he experienced while riding on horseback near Holyoke, Colorado, in the winter of 1931. NUFORC investigators were so impressed by the story, director Peter Davenport said that they contacted the witness by telephone and spent a long time discussing the sighting with him. "We spoke with the witness at length, and he seemed to us to be exceptionally reliable and credible," Davenport said.

The witness did not know the exact date but estimated it was sometime in February of 1931. He was 17 years old at the time and had been assigned the job of riding his horse out to a pasture after a snowstorm to inspect the cattle. The location was a ranch located about eight miles southwest of the town of Holyoke, Colorado.

The witness rode his horse over a small hill and then down to a draw [a dry creek or stream] that was about 25 to 30 feet deep. Heading toward the south, he moved along the draw until he got to about its halfway point, when he suddenly saw a very strange sight.

Man on Horseback (Library of Congress)

Looking up to the west, the witness saw "an elongated oval shaped flying machine" moving through the air with ease. It was the color of aluminum.

Remaining atop his horse, the witness continued observing the strange airship. While he was looking at it, he saw what appeared to be an open doorway in the flying vessel. Through the open door, which he assumed was covered by glass, he noticed a "dark" humanoid looking down at him.

"A man appeared that looked human but was not as tall as a normal human," the witness said. Also, the humanoid was wearing a uniform that seemed even darker than he was. As far as encounters with occupants of flying saucers go, this was a rather brief one – but interesting. The "dark" appearance of the humanoid may have been attributable to the lighting inside the ship. The witness may have been seeing the creature silhouetted against the lighted backdrop of the ship's interior. Interestingly, the humanoid's uniform seemed "darker" than the rest of the figure.

UFO Illustration by Patrick Fischer from Pixabay

At this point in the observation of this phenomenon, the witness's horse stumbled a bit, and he was forced to look down at the animal, turning his gaze away from the fascinating object just for a moment. When he turned his attention back up to the UFO, the object had disappeared in an instant. There was absolutely no trace of it left anywhere in the immediate vicinity.

SAN PEDRO MOUNTAINS MUMMY

San Pedro Mountains, Wyoming
1932

OUR STORY BEGINS OFF in the San Pedro Mountains in the hot summer months of 1932. That July, Cecil Main and Frank Carr were mining for gold in the mountains. While tracing a seam of gold into the rock face of the mountain they ran into a literal dead end. They had no choice but to blast into the rock face. To their disappointment, when the smoke cleared, they found no more gold. However, the explosion had revealed a hidden cave within the mountain. The cave measured four feet wide and fifteen feet long. Within it, they found an object that was quite possibly otherworldly. Sitting cross-legged on a ledge was a tiny mummy only six inches tall. It had been mummified from the natural elements over time, and as such most of its features were still intact and discernable. And what strange features they were. A gelatinous substance covered the head, and the facial features were odd with a low, flat forehead and flattened nose. Then there were the rather bulbous eyes and the full set of teeth—we point out the teeth because if the tiny six inch mummy was a fetus as some argue, then it shouldn't have had teeth.

MUMMIFIED PYGMY FOUND

LUSK, Wyo.—(U.P)—A mummified pygmy, believed by scientists to be a progenitor of the present human race, was exhibited in Lusk recently. The mummy is owned by Homer F. Sherrill, of Crawford, Neb., and has baffled scientists in various parts of the country where it has been sent for classification. It was unearthed in a cave on a slope of one of the Peaks of Pedro mountain, near Casper, Wyo.

Article About the 1932 San Pedro Mummy

Though they were still disappointed by the lack of gold, Main and Carr knew they could still make a profit off of the mummy in exhibitions. For instance, at the time, the mummified carcass of a man alleged to be John Wilkes Booth was a popular attraction at carnivals and circuses. So it certainly wasn't unusual in the era for curiosities such as that to hit the road or be part of a traveling cabinet of curiosities.

Due to being found in the San Pedro Mountains, they nicknamed their little mummy Pedro and took him to Casper, Wyoming, about 60 miles away. It's unknown if Main and Carr exhibited the carcass themselves, or if they sold it right away to a carnival barker. All we know is that it toured around Wyoming for two years up until 1936, when it was purchased by Meeteetse drug store owner Floyd Jones, who put the mummy in his display window to entice customers to come inside.

Somehow, Pedro made his way back to Casper and into the sales room of a car dealership owned by Ivan Goodman. With a flare for showmanship, he touted that, "It's educational! It's Scientific! It will amaze and thrill you. It's a pygmy preserved as it actually lived!" Goodman made up a story that the mummy was thousands of years old, and a distant ancestor of the human race. However, others think that the mummy could have come from a race beyond the stars. As it stands, Native American myths telling of advanced little people are not uncommon. We covered a case wherein Lewis and Clark learned of a race of what the Native Americans called "little devils" who stood eighteen inches high and had large heads in comparison to their bodies.

Little Pedro would seem to have died a violent death unbefitting of a little baby, as his skull appeared to have been smashed along with a broken collarbone and a damaged spine. Of course, it could have been an accident, but what if

Pedro was one of the war-like little people who died in combat?

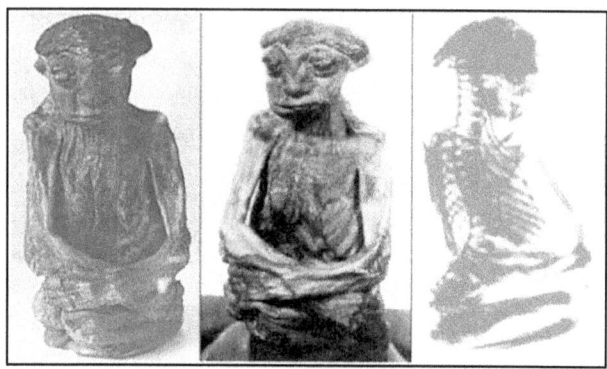

The 1932 San Pedro Mummy

Some have thought Pedro is one of the mythical Nimerigar peoples. This race of little people lived in the vicinity of Wind River and the San Pedro Mountains. According to myth, the Nimerigar stood anywhere between 20 inches and three feet in height. [The three-foot height is interesting as that's about the right size for a Grey alien.] Like the little people that Lewis and Clark heard of, the Nimerigar were not to be trifled with, as they were not only violent, but also had magic powers. As for the powers, the Nez Perce tribe alleged that the beings could turn themselves invisible with a special grass. The Shoshone considered the little people to be tricksters, and blamed most of their bad luck on them. Similar to the Nimerigar were another tribe called the Nirumbee, which would sometimes abduct children. The violent aspect of the Nimerigar would seem to fit in with Pedro's violent death as it was said that the Nimerigar would kill the elderly with a blow to the skull when they outlived their usefulness.

Pedro was at one point x-rayed by the American Museum of Natural History in New York and these x-rays were later verified by the Anthropology Department of Harvard University. Though the results proved that Pedro was an actual mummy, and not a cobbled-together hoax, the question still remained: what was it? Of course, no one from that era would stop to propose it may have come from space, as aliens were still not a part of the public conscious. Not that any respectable scientific institution would ever endorse the belief in aliens at that time, either. As far as scientists were concerned, Pedro must have been a baby suffering from a rare genetic condition known as anencephaly. The unfortunate condition occurs in the womb and often results in the absence of part of the fetus's brain, skull, and scalp, which seemed to match Pedro's case. Or, at least, that was the most logical explanation scientists could agree upon before drifting to the dreaded realm of myth and legend, which is never afforded the proper respect among scientists.

You may now be asking why proper testing hasn't been conducted on Pedro recently? That's because, unfortunately, Pedro mysteriously disappeared in the 1950s. It is thought that Goodman, the car salesman, sold him to what some call a "New York con man". According to David Weatherly in *Monsters of Big Sky Country*, the New York man was named Leonard Walder, and the mummy only vanished upon Walder's death in the 1980s.

One almost has to wonder if the mummy is really lost, or if the problematic mummy was carted off by someone within the government...

UNDERGROUND CITY OF THE LIZARD PEOPLE

Los Angeles, California
1933-1934

EARLIER IN THIS BOOK, we established the concepts of both Reptilian aliens (in the chapter on Robert E. Howard) and underground alien cities (in several chapters dealing with Nazi beliefs). 1930s-era Los Angeles is probably one of the last places one would expect to have ties to Reptilians, but if newspaper stories from 1933-1934 are to be believed, it has a big one. According to newspaper reports that began in late 1933, Los Angeles sat on top of an underground city built by the "Lizard People". The first article began by stating,

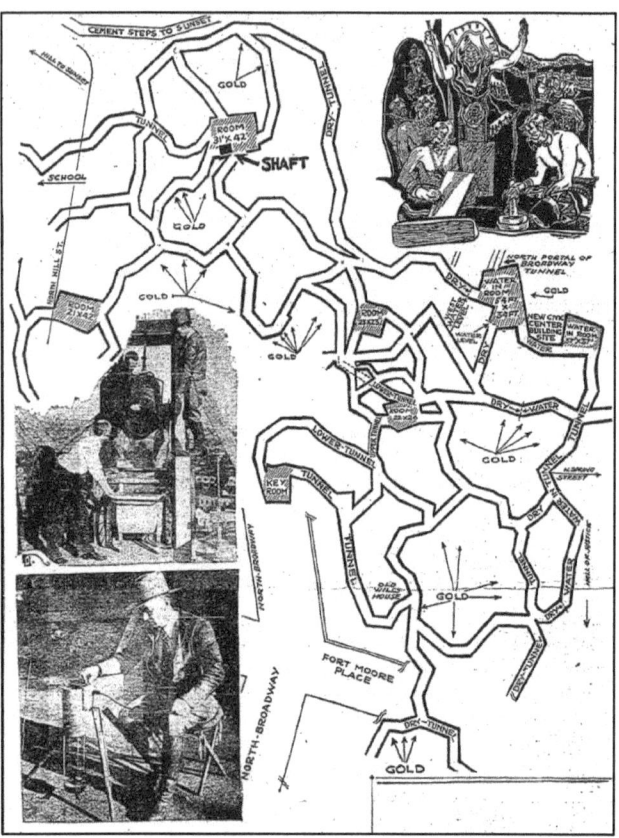

Image Accompanying the Original Article.

Busy Los Angeles, although little realizing it in the hustle and bustle of modern existence, stands above a lost city of catacombs filled with incalculable treasure and imperishable records of a race of humans further advanced intellectually and scientifically than even the highest type of present day peoples, in the belief of G. Warren Shufelt, geophysical mining engineer now engaged in an attempt to wrest from the lost city deep in the earth below Fort Moore Hill the secrets of the Lizard People of legendary fame in the medicine lodges of the American Indian.

The story went on to claim that these Lizard People escaped a cataclysmic meteor shower by hiding underground. This matches up with many Native American creation myths. According to both Native Americans and Mesoamericans alike, the world has been destroyed and recreated about four times. The last devastation was the famous flood common to cultures across the world. But, before that, the earth was destroyed by fire from the sky, which sounds an awful lot like meteors.

Specifically, the article mentioned how the Lizard People survived a great catastrophe about 5,000 years ago and went on to say,

This legendary catastrophe was in the form of a huge tongue of fire which "came out of the Southwest, destroying all life in its path," the path being "several hundred miles wide." The city underground was dug as a means of escaping future fires ... Large rooms in the domes of the hills above the city of labyrinths housed 1,000 families "in the manner of tall buildings" and imperishable food supplies of the herb variety were stored in the catacombs to provide sustenance for the lizard folk for great lengths of time ...

BURIED FORTUNE HUNT TO BEGIN

Quest to Start on Fort Moore Hill

[A. P. photo]

If "Doodlebugs" Don't Lie, Here's Where
Left to right—Rex Irving McCreery and O. Warren Shufelt, with the
electrical radio gold-finding machine.

*Rare Photo of Shufelt (Right) and One of his
Compatriots, Rex Irving.*

One of the Original Articles

A more detailed article, "Lizard People's Catacomb City Hunted" by Jean Bosquet, appeared in the *Los Angeles Times* on January 29, 1934. It elaborated on the mining engineer G. Warren Shufelt mentioned in the first article. Shufelt believed that somewhere under the vicinity of "the old Banning property on North Hill Street overlooking Sunset Boulevard, Spring Street and North Broadway" that "a maze of catacombs and priceless golden tablets" could be found. The article in full is as follows:

LOS ANGELES. Jan. 30. (IP). Indian legend and a "radio x-ray" have started a group of men digging in the heart of Los Angeles for a lost underground city of the lizard people. The shaft, now down 250 feet, the explorers believe, will lead to the "key room" of the city of catacombs in which were stored the city records, written on tablets of gold. G. Warren Shufelt, geophysical mining engineer and designer of the x-ray, and other associates dug 50 feet on county property in the same area not long ago looking for gold supposed to have been buried by Spaniards. The county denied them a permit to dig further. But Shufelt continued explorations with his device, which led him hither and yon over an area from the public library to the Southwest Museum. "I knew I was over a pattern of tunnels," he declared today, "and had mapped out their course, the position of large rooms and the location of deposits of gold, but I couldn't understand the meaning of it." He was taken to Little Chief Greenleaf, an educated Hopi Indian from Arizona who sometimes lectures under the English name of L. Macklin. Shufelt said Macklin told him he apparently had located one of three lost cities on the Pacific Coast dug by the lizard people about 5,000 years ago after a great tongue of fire had "come out of the southwest destroying all life in its path." They dug the labyrinths to escape future fires and one of the cities lay within a chain of hills forming "the frog of a horse's hoof." The description fit, said Shufelt, and he interested other persons in financing the shaft, which is being dug on North Hill street within a few blocks of the city hall. The legend, as told by Macklin to Shufelt, said the lost city was dug with powerful chemicals by the lizard people. The tunnels began at the ocean and the tide, passing daily in and out of the lower portals, forced air into the upper tunnels providing ventilation. Large rooms in the domes of hills housed hundreds of families, who stored imperishable food supplies of the herb variety against the coming of another fire. The lizard people, who were reputed to be highly intellectual and to have developed a cement better than any now in use, regarded the lizard as the symbol of long life. They laid their city out in the shape of one, its tail to the southwest. "The legendary story must remain speculative," said Shufelt, "until proved by excavation."

CATACOMBS UNDER CITY DECLARED GOLD-FILLED

Catacombs under Los Angeles.

And gold in them thar hills—or in thet thar hill, to be more specific.

This is the gist of a report to Supervisor Shaw's office by Rex Irving McCreery and G. Warren Shufelt, who, together with Roy Martin, were engaged in seeking buried treasure beneath the rounded surface of old Fort Moore Hill back of the Hall of Justice.

The hunt for old Spanish doubloons and bullion was launched after Shufelt, owner of a radio device with which he asserts he can locate gold deposits, made a preliminary survey of the hill some months ago.

Martin possesses an old Spanish map which also indicates the eminence is the hiding place of forgotten treasure, and on the strength of Shufelt's findings and Martin's chart a contract was entered into with the county giving the men permission to seek gold. The county was to collect 30 per cent royalty on anything they found.

The contract has expired and the search has ceased, at least temporarily, without the three treasure seekers or the county being any the richer except in experience as the result of a month's digging.

But the erstwhile gold-diggers are not to be discouraged.

In petitioning the Board of Supervisors for an extension of their contract, Shufelt stated he has completed a very thorough survey of the hill with his radio contraption and has arrived at the following conclusions:

Fort Moore Hill hides a labyrinth of tunnels with a total length of 1900 feet and rooms embracing 9000 square feet of floor space. There are at least sixteen places where gold is buried or concealed in vaults.

The board will consider extending the contract today.

Unfortunately, this is where the story ends, as there were no follow-up articles either proving or disproving the story. A variation of the article above did mention that Shufelt planned "to continue sending his shaft downward until he has reached a depth of 1000 feet before discontinuing operations."

A 2014 article on the dig, "The Underground Catacombs of L.A.'s Lizard People" by Glen Creason for *Los Angeles Magazine* related that the dig was brought to halt by huge boulders and too much mud as the depths increased. Apparently, Shufelt gave up in the Spring of 1934 when his funding dried up and passed away in North Hollywood in November of 1957.

Though no concrete evidence of the city was ever found, it's still an intriguing story in the realm of potential extraterrestrial encampments on Earth. Chief Greenleaf's claim that the Lizard Men dug the tunnels with powerful chemicals is eyebrow raising. Where would they even get an idea like that if the story was made up? Why not simply say the Lizard People dug the tunnels, but Greenleaf implied super-scientific knowledge. In any case, tales of an advanced race of peoples with ties to reptiles certainly tie in with mentions of the "Great Old Ones" mentioned earlier in the chapter on Robert E. Howard.

In June of 1994, *Unsolved Mysteries* investigated the story and brought in a team of skilled professionals to investigate the areas where the Lizard City was located. Robert Stack narrated that, "Incredibly the sensitive instruments revealed that the legendary treasures of Elysian Park may in fact be real."

GOLD HUNT RESUMES AT OLD FORT

Supervisors Renew Permit to Diggers in Quest of Spanish Treasure

The hunt for Spanish gold supposedly buried in a maze of catacombs under old Fort Moore Hill is scheduled to be resumed with new vigor this week following action of the Board of Supervisors in granting a renewal of the contract under which the search was started more than a month ago.

Under the terms of the contract the gold-seekers, Rex Irving McCreery, G. Warren Shufelt and Roy Martin, will have another thirty days in which to dig holes to a depth of fifty feet in their quest for the bullion and catacombs they claim constitute a large part of the innards of the old Los Angeles landmark.

The first month of digging under the original contract produced nothing more than sore backs, blistered hands, a twenty-six-foot hole and a copious mound of removed earth for the gold hunters and the county. In the meantime, Shufelt, whose radio-electric doodlebug's palpitations provided the incentive for the treasure search, reported that he had made a new survey of the hill and is convinced that it conceals a vast maze of masonried catacombs and millions in bullion deposits, hidden here and there.

The contract calls for a fifty-fifty split with the county on anything that is found in the diggin's.

Today, most people gloss over the Reptilian connection, arguing that the "Lizard People" were simply an advanced race of human beings who worshiped the lizard. However, researcher David Weatherly found an interesting tie between Los Angeles's underground city and true, alien Reptilians. Weatherly, in his book *Copper State Monsters*, cites from the article to make a connection between the Reptilians of the Superstition Mountains in Arizona and the Lizard People of L.A.

Weatherly has collected stories from Apache descendants in the Superstition Mountains who claim to have seen huge "two-legged lizard men". The implication was not a remnant dinosaur sighting, however, but that of a Reptilian (key word "lizard men").

"Over the years, I've heard many accounts... stories of lizard people, or as they're known 'reptilians' or 'reptoids', who live in the mountains and present a danger to any who trespass in their territory," Weatherly wrote on page 182 of *Copper State Monsters*. Furthermore, the older tribes of Apache warned the Spanish Conquistadors not to go into the mountains for fear of gods and monsters, which some speculate might have been the Lizard People. And these so-called Lizard People might very well be the same ones who dug the alleged city beneath Los Angeles...

TRIANGLE UFO IN ALASKA

Eklutna, Alaska
October 15, 1936

ON FEBRUARY 5, 2001, a fascinating UFO report was submitted to the National UFO Reporting Center (NUFORC) by the widow of the recently deceased Holger Berg (1917-2001). Prior to his death on January 27, 2001, at age 83, Berg had told his story verbally to NUFORC investigators, who had encouraged him to write it out in narrative form. What follows is Berg's amazing story.

In the fall of 1936, the 19-year-old Berg was in Alaska, working for the Washington Fish & Oyster Company at their cannery on Shuyak Island, known as Port Williams. He worked both as a general mechanic and at making cans for the salmon canning operation, using equipment made by the Continental Can Company. Berg made the cans and then checked them to ensure that they were sealing properly. It was a job he enjoyed, but, unfortunately for him, it was seasonal.

An Alaska Salmon Cannery in the 1930s

When the salmon season ended, as did his job at the cannery, Berg signed on to work for the Civilian Conservation Corp. He was assigned to help establish a camp at Eklutna, 27 miles north of Anchorage, located on a major highway. The camp was the construction site of Eklutna's power plan buildings.

Berg's co-workers included about ten other young men, most of whom were from the eastern United States, such as New Hampshire, Vermont, and Massachusetts. The group of workers endured constant cold, ranging from 20 to 25 degrees Fahrenheit, and up to ten inches of snow on the ground.

The young men all slept in a large bunkhouse, and their free time was spent gathered around a coal burning stove, playing cards, reading, or just talking. Berg remembered, "Weekends were long, and the biggest activity was chucking coal in the stove. Everyone took turns to keep the fire going the night."

The UFO incident happened on one particular Saturday night when Berg and a co-worker, named Peterson, decided to leave camp and hitch a ride to nearby Anchorage, where they planned to see a movie. Their plan was ridiculed by the other workers, who thought they were insane for braving the freezing cold weather at night just for a movie.

"The two of us started out," Berg remembered. "The sky was pitch black, with the stars glistening like jewels, and the air was still."

Walking at a brisk pace along the highway, hoping that a car would come along and offer them a ride, the two men eventually covered a distance of about four or five miles when they heard an unearthly sound and saw an intense bluish light that seemed to be coming toward them on the highway. They thought it was a truck with one headlight burned out. Berg said, "The sound we heard was like the sound of a jet turbine being shut down -- not a high-pitched sound." (Berg worked for the Boeing Aircraft Company in later years.)

The men soon realized that the bluish light was not traveling along the road, but rather was hovering in the air. When the men understood this, they were startled and frightened. Within a few minutes, the object was upon them, and they flattened themselves out on the snow, as it whooshed past them overhead.

It appeared to be a cigar-shaped craft with a bluish light attached to its side. It didn't seem like a very large object at first, but later, as it moved farther away, Berg realized that he had not seen the full extent of the craft. It was much wider than he originally thought.

A Flatiron

National Gallery of Art, CC0, via Wikimedia Commons

In David Marler's 2013 book *Triangular UFOs: An Estimate of the Situation,* Berg is quoted as saying, "It looked like it was cigar shaped. However, as it got away from us, it looked more like a flatiron. You know it [was] wider at the back than it was at the front. I'm sure that we had that in our sights [for] over three minutes. Cause it was not moving very fast and it was less than 1000 feet. And this is the part that really frightened us. When I think about it, there may have been more than one light, but it was one blue green light or maybe a couple of them either on the sides or on the top."

In Marler's book, NUFORC director Peter Davenport said, "What began to trouble them is that as the object drew closer was that its shape was distinctly triangular, similar in appearance to that of a flatiron, used for ironing clothes. Moreover, it appeared to them to be embedded in a 'cloud' of blue-green light, a color they had never seen before.... As the object passed almost directly over them, the two men were able to confirm the triangular shape of the ventral surface of the craft. As it flew away from them, the witnesses could see some type of peculiar, multi-colored lighting on its aft end."

After the close encounter, Berg said, "Peterson and I were now standing up looking at the object heading east. It was headed toward a mountain or high foothills. As we kept looking at it, we both thought it would crash into the mountain. It seemed to lift up and went over and down the other side. We looked at each other and exclaimed, 'What the hell was that?' We decided to return to the Camp, which we did, wondering what it was we had seen."

NUFORC director Peter Davenport was very impressed by the testimony of Mr. Berg. He said, "We spoke with Mr. Berg on many occasions about his sighting, and we found his story to be most compelling."

Depiction of UFO by PhotoVision from Pixabay

POSSIBLE ALIEN ABDUCTION

Fontana, California
Summer 1937 or 1938

IN ANOTHER INTERESTING CASE from the archives of the National UFO Reporting Center (NUFORC), in 1937 or 1938, a youth we will refer to as "Harry" and two of his brothers encountered a brightly lit cylindrical UFO that hovered directly above them for up to ten minutes. One of the witnesses, for years afterward, had "dreams" of being aboard the UFO and being poked and prodded by small humanoids with large heads and large eyes.

The story begins with Harry and his brothers leaving their small residence on the outskirts of Fontana, California, and walking into town to watch a movie in the downtown area. As this was the height of the Great Depression, the family was very poor and lived in an isolated "old tractor barn."

The movie ended at around 9 p.m., and the boys headed back home, walking down an old two-lane road without streetlights. It was a very dark night, and there was no traffic at all on the road.

Fontana Movie Theater, Built in 1937
By Jordan W., CC BY-SA 3.0, via Wikimedia

In his NUFORC report, Harry remembered, "We were just talking and walking as three young boys will do, when to our surprise, the brightest light that we had ever seen came on right above us; it was cylinder in shape; it was like we were in a bright glass [tube]."

The object hovering above them shone an intensely bright light on the boys, totally bathing them in light and making them feel as though they were inside a glass enclosure. There was a sensation of being trapped or "frozen" within a tube of light.

For a length of time that Harry later guessed was around ten minutes, nothing happened. Then suddenly, the three boys, in a panicked reaction, ran away from under the hovering UFO and into a nearby orange grove, where they hid under orange trees.

Grove of Orange Trees
by Hans Braxmeier from Pixabay

Much to their terror, the UFO also moved toward their new location, shining its intense light all around the trees under which they were hiding. Harry said, "It was brighter than daylight under the orange tree that I was under. We were yelling at each other and really scared by this time."

In the horror and panic of the moment, the boys felt that they were in mortal danger and that they might not survive the ordeal. At the same time, they had not an inkling of a clue as to what force they were facing. "We didn't know what to do," Harry said.

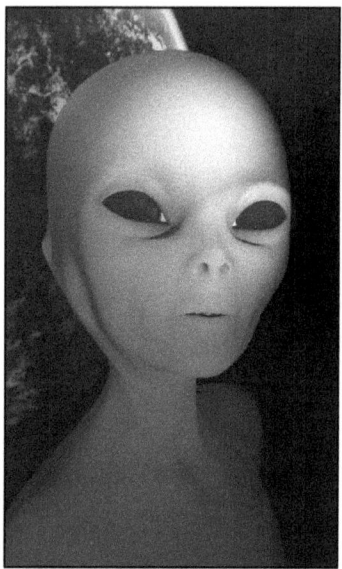

Depiction of Alien ^{by Borkia from Pixabay}

Then suddenly, the intense light bathing the trees around them switched off just as quickly as it had turned on. "We stayed under the trees and talked back and forth to each other until we got up enough nerve to get up and run."

As the years passed, the three witnesses refrained from telling others of their experience, concerned that they would be ridiculed or laughed at. As Harry said in his NUFORC report, 1937/1938 was a time when nobody had ever heard of UFOs or aliens.

And then the strange "dreams" began haunting Harry. "For a long time after that event, I had what I thought were dreams. I would awake in room with subdued light, with four or five of the little people with the big head and eyes, they always looked light blue or green or grey to me. They would be moving all around and touching me."

Although Harry did not disclose this incident until 2002, it appears to be a significant case with many of the features of later UFO sightings and abduction cases. Is it possible that the three boys were abducted and brought aboard the hovering craft at some point during their ordeal? It certainly could be the case. Or perhaps Harry was somehow tracked by the UFO occupants and then visited in later years.

He was concerned about being visited by the ETs because of the remote location of his residence. "This was during the Great Depression and we lived in an old tractor barn with very few people near us."

The "dreams" continued, according to Harry: "In this dream that I used to have, once in a while a door would open with a bright light, and in the doorway would be this tall man. I could never tell what he looked like; all I could see was his shadow. He would say something to the little people and soon after, I would awake in my bed."

"I was never too afraid of them, I can't ever recall being hurt in any way," Harry said.

After thinking about what happened to him for many years, he finally decided that it was not dreams he was having. By the time he filed his report with NUFORC, he said, "The older I get, the more I think there is more to my story than I thought. All of the people that say they have seen the same thing ... can't be telling stories."

NUFORC director Peter Davenport said, "What a wonderful, and interesting, report!"

Although the boys mentioned in the NUFORC report were not identified, UFO researcher Cheryl Costa wrote an article about the case in 2017 that identified the principal witness as "Harry" and the other two boys with him as his brothers. Costa's article "A Close Encounter In 1937 Fontana," appeared in the *Syracuse (N.Y.) New Times.*

TARZAN AUTHOR VISITS BROTHER

(By International News Service)
FONTANA, April 1.—Edgar Rice Burroughs, author of the Tarzan books, and his family were recent visitors at the home of his brother, G. T. Burroughs, on South Cypress street, Fontana.

The San Bernardino (Calif.) County Sun, 4-2-1937, p. 14.

In an interesting sidenote to this story, Fontana, California, in the 1930s was often visited by world-famous American science-fiction writer Edgar Rice

Burroughs, author of the *John Carter of Mars* books and the *Tarzan of the Apes* series. He visited Fontana to spend time with his brother, G.T. Burroughs, who lived in Fontana at that time.

1917 Cover of A Princess of Mars *by Edgar Rice Burroughs*

In terms of other possible alien abductions in the 1930s, documentation is unfortunately lacking. What follows is a small slice of the other reported UFO abductions, which would greatly benefit from additional research verification. However, these short tales are all much too fascinating to leave out of the book.

The first of these additional cases begins in the year 1919 with a man by the name of Mike Childers, who was backpacking—or hoboing as it was called in those days—across the country. He arrived in the vicinity of Tehachapi, California, where he decided to camp in the woods for the night. When he awoke the next morning, he was seemingly still in the same spot, but he did not realize until later that much more time had elapsed than he was first aware of. As he resumed his trek across the country, he noticed that things seemed strangely different. Eventually, he figured out that it was now the year 1934, meaning it had been fifteen years since he fell asleep at his campsite! This is certainly one of the most extreme cases of missing time ever, and it's important to clarify that not only could Childers not remember the missing fifteen years, but his body did not seem to have aged at all! He was as young as he was back in 1919.

According to several UFO authors and researchers, Childers made a "small media splash as a modern-day Rip Van Winkle," a reference to the 1819 novel by Washington Irving about a man who falls asleep and awakens twenty years later. Unfortunately, we could not independently verify this incident by locating primary reference sources from the 1930s; however, the story does appear in a number of UFO tales collected by other researchers.

But the Childers story doesn't end there. In 1990, the elderly Childers began to have nightmares that seemed to hint at the root of his missing time experience. Supposedly, Childers saw Dr. Denton Schaeffer on "a tabloid talk show" about repressed memories and wrote to him about his experience. To bolster his credibility, Childers made sure to include some newspaper articles about himself from the 1930s in the letter.

Vintage Postcard Depicting Rip Van Winkle.

Schaeffer agreed to meet Childers and eventually put him under hypnosis. During one of his hypnosis sessions, Childers recalled memories of being taken underground by strange, chattering alien creatures. In the visions, Childers recalled undergoing a kind of brain surgery and being transported to "alien realms". To back this up,

Childers underwent a medical exam that reportedly proved he had endured some kind of cranial surgery many years ago. Childers died in 1995.

Another 1930s UFO abduction case occurred in the Arizona Desert in 1938 and was unearthed by researcher Brad Steiger, whose work is similar to John Keel's. Steiger managed to dig up the account of a gentleman named Steve Brodie, who was out with a friend one afternoon in the desert searching for gems. Suddenly, Brodie heard his friend utter a scream. He looked up to see a black-cowled figure standing at the base of a nearby mesa. This humanoid was joined by another dark figure, and after this it pointed a strange wand-like device at Brodie. He was immediately stricken with paralysis, and when his friend attempted to run, he too was stricken by the wand. Only, in this case, it had a different effect, as Brodie said he could hear his friend scream, and that the air was filled with the smell of burnt flesh, suggesting his friend had been burned.

Then a third humanoid approached Brodie with a set of what we would today call earphones. At this point, Brodie blacked out, and all he could remember were brief bouts of consciousness where he recalled himself being kept in a cage-like enclosure with other humans. Every time Brodie would begin to come out of his stupor, one of the beings would approach him with the rod again, and he would blackout. The next thing he knew, Brodie found himself wandering in the streets of New York City near Time Square. This account was published in Steiger's book, *Monsters Among Us.*

Another interesting alien encounter occurred in 1938, and this one has more credibility because it happened to current day UFO researcher Raymond Fowler. As a young boy at the age of six in Danvers, Massachusetts, Fowler had strange reoccurring dreams of a dark figure

Raymond E. Fowler
(Courtesy Jerry Pippin)

appearing in his room. Preceding the figure's appearance, he would feel "a strange electric like tingling sensation." When he tried to cry out to his parents, he found that he was struck with paralysis and could not. The figure, to his horror, would come closer and closer to him, and that would be where the recollection would end.

As it turned out, Fowler's father had also had at least one encounter with otherworldly humanoids as documented in our book *UFOs in the Roaring Twenties.* The elder Fowler's encounter occurred at Mount Desert Island, Maine, when he was a radioman in charge of the naval station in 1923. In this case, a violent electrical storm caused Fowler to be struck with electricity from a lightning strike in the control room. Three seemingly benevolent humanoids in robes appeared to him and removed the harmful electricity from his body!

UFOs OF THE TURBULENT THIRTIES

Though the beings in the elder Fowler's case were there to help as opposed to the being that tormented the younger Fowler, it's interesting to note that electricity seemed to play a role in both encounters.

ALIENS IN THE PORTHOLES

Somerville, Massachusetts
Summer 1938

IN A CASE published in the 1969 book *UFO: The Whole Story* by Coral & Jim Lorenzen, an eyewitness named Malcolm B. Perry (1913-2014) told of a highly unusual sighting he experienced in the summer of 1938 in Somerville, Massachusetts.

The witness himself is notable, as he was the son of renowned American landscape artist Frank C. Perry. An artist himself, Malcolm's paintings hang in many private collections. He was also a body builder, Judo enthusiast, and an accomplished herbologist. Living to age 100, he attributed his long life to the use of medicinal herbs and the avoidance of pharmaceuticals.

UFO Researchers Jim & Coral Lorenzen,
1955 Photo

On a summer night in 1938, the 25-year-old was outdoors when he saw a strange object approaching his position from the east. He thought, at first, that it was a blimp, but as it drew nearer, he saw that it had no gondola or propeller of any kind.

Observing closely, Perry saw that the airship had several "portholes" along the side that was facing him. These portholes were backlit by some sort of internal illumination, and at one of these portholes, he noticed the silhouette of a humanoid figure in a sitting position. The impression Perry got was that the strange humanoid was intently looking down at him.

As the sighting continued, Perry noticed a number of other "people" moving around inside the ship, revealing themselves as they moved across the portholes.

Illustration of UFO with Portholes and Silhouetted Figures (Art by Joe Calkins)

At one point during the sighting, Perry felt a strong impulse to wave at the humanoids in the passing airship. He felt an overwhelming sensation of friendliness toward them, "as if they were old friends."

Eventually, the strange craft moved into a bank of clouds and could not be seen any longer. It did not reappear after that.

What Malcolm Perry saw on that summer day in 1938 remains a mystery to this day. Since he was an artist, it would be interesting to discover if he ever drew or sketched any images of the UFO that he observed. There have been no such images ever made public, unfortunately, but perhaps someday, his family may discover a sketch among his personal belongings.

In an obituary that appeared in The Quincy, Massachusetts, *Patriot Ledger* on January 29, 2014, the following appears:

Malcolm B. Perry of Dorchester, 100 years, passed away Jan. 25, after a brief illness. He was the devoted husband of the late Muriel (Caiger); loving father of the late John F. Perry and Virginia A. Perry. Survived by sons, Robert A. Perry and wife Janice (Salemmi) of Marshfield and Richard F. Perry of Dorchester. He was the extra-loving Grandpa of nine grandchildren and seven great-grandchildren. Mr. Perry was the son of renowned American landscape and seascape artist Frank C. Perry. Mr. Perry was born in Putnam, Conn., Aug. 26,1913. Upon completion of high school, Mr. Perry attended and graduated from the Scott Carbee School of Art in Boston. As an artist his paintings hang in many private collections. His mural behind the baptismal at Dorchester Temple Baptist Church is one his largest canvases. As a young man he studied body building at the Y.M.C.A. There he would give Judo demonstrations to the cadets of the Boston Police Department. He was also an accomplished herbologist. He studied the medicinal use of plants and herbs and many people approached him for his advice on the subject. He attributed his long life to use of said herbs and the avoidance of institutional medicine.

INVASION OF THE FIREBALLS

Various Locations
1930-1934

STRANGE FIREBALLS, often mistaken for meteors, have been observed throughout human history, with the 1930s being no exception. In this chapter, we will examine some of the most impressive "fireball" sightings of the decade. These objects have long been considered a type of UFO.

In the spring of either 1930 or 1931, a high school student named Ralph Newman was walking along a country road near Newberry, Michigan at about 7 p.m., when he noticed a bright green object moving from south to north, low in the eastern sky. As the object arced across the sky, its illumination brightened the countryside, almost like a full moon does.

Newman was startled by the sighting and later described it as a "distinctly green fireball" that moved across the sky for about 20 degrees before it simply "vanished into thin air."

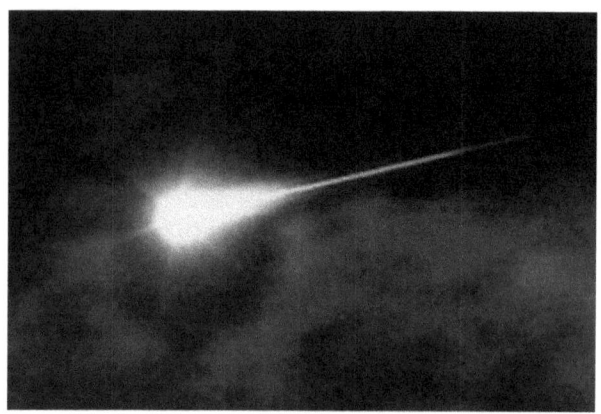

Fireball Image (Wikimedia Commons)

The size of the object, Newman said, was a bit smaller than the apparent size of the moon, except that its color was green. The object made no sound at all as it moved and then disappeared.

The sighting came to light in 1952 and has been reported by UFO researcher Jerome Clark in his work *The UFO Encyclopedia: The Phenomenon from the Beginning.*

On August 9, 1934, at about 5 a.m., Leon Thompson was boating on Keuka Lake in Western New York, when he noticed an odd-looking, cone-shaped cloud on the west side of the lake. The cloud looked like an elongated cone about 60-75 feet in length and about 10-15 feet in diameter at its largest point.

Suddenly, the sky above the lake lit up in a flash, and out of the strange cloud came a fireball that streaked across the lake in an arc to the east, leaving a fiery trail behind it.

The fireball fell toward the ground and struck a nearby cottage, spewing up a cloud of mist or steam. The mist lingered for minutes before it slowly dissipated.

The incident was reported in the 2015 book *Return to Magonia: Investigating UFOs in History,* by Chris Aubeck and Martin Slough.

In Oakland, California, on a summer evening in 1932 or 1933, two teenagers on their way to a Boy Scout meeting observed seven or eight fireballs "all flying in a bunch" over the Oakland hills to the east.

The witnesses were Fred Van Sant and his brother Milton. Fred later said, "We stared at them in amazement for we knew that meteors didn't fly in bunches. Also, these didn't seem to fall toward the earth, but maintained the same altitude, which seemed very high, and flew in a great arc as though they were on a great circle route."

Fred described them as "bright points of light like the planet Venus," except that there was a "flame" emanating from the back end of each fireball. They were so bright that they seemed to be emitting their own light. The witnesses could not hear any sound.

The objects first appeared at an angle of about 30 degrees in the east and flew toward the west at around 45 degrees. They remained in the same relative position during the time that the boys observed them.

UFOs OF THE TURBULENT THIRTIES

In 1933, on the Wind River Indian Reservation near Fort Washakie, Wyoming, a truck with two occupants had just crested a hill when the men inside observed three perfectly round, pulsating orange-red balls about 900 feet away from the truck and slightly below them.

One of the witnesses said, "From our position, we were looking almost down on these objects which were moving slowly in absolute alignment towards the nearest mountain range."

The objects seemed to be about 20 feet off the ground and appeared to emit a pulsating light. There was absolutely no sound. After the occupants of the truck observed the strange objects for about five minutes, the fireballs disappeared over a nearby mountain.

On July 31 or August 1, 1933, at about 9:15 p.m., California high school science teacher Paul M. Berry, Jr., was sky-watching when he saw two strange fireballs shoot across the sky. The sighting occurred in a wilderness area between the Humbug Valley and Butt Reservoir Valley in Northern California.

Berry described the two objects as "each more a prolate spheroid than lenticular, with blunt ends." Although they appeared to be solid and clearly outlined, they were surrounded by a "considerable green luminescence."

Berry observed no pieces flaking off or detaching from the fireballs. He saw no smoke or trail. The brightness of the objects diminished as they approached the horizon.

Berry estimated that the objects were about 8-10 miles away from him, and their size was comparable to that of a nickel held at arm's length – or maybe slightly larger.

Unusual Green Fireballs Recently Seen In Southwest May Be Missiles

ALBUQUERQUE (AP)—Dr. Lincoln la Paz said today the unusual green fireballs observed over the Southwest recently could be guided missiles—our own or somebody else's.

The meteor specialist of the University of New Mexico gave three possible explanations of the fireballs that startled residents of the Southwest over a two-week period.

"They may be simply an unconventional kind of meteoritic fireball. They may be guided missiles undergoing a test in the area which they are designed to defend, or they may be guided missiles of foreign origin."

Dr. La Paz said the latter two

explanations should "not be cast aside too hastily in the Buck Rogers era which mankind has entered."

Guided missile tests, either by friend or foe, would probably be designed to give the impression that the guided missiles emanated from known meteoritic radiants in order to cloud their true nature, he said.

La Paz added, "The fact that the military intelligence expert, Col. C. H. Lanza, went on record in the 'Field Artillery Journal' with observations of green fireballs traversing in the sky above the Baltic and Sweden as long ago as 1946 and mentions the possible explanation of them as being test firing by Russians of guided missiles . . . should not be overlooked in attempts to evaluate green fireball sightings."

The Index-Journal (Greenwood, S.C.), 1-2-1952, p. 7

After the first two objects passed from view in about five seconds, a third, identical UFO came into view, following the same path as the first two.

In June of 1932, Reuben Knight stood on his porch looking across a meadow at his farm near Wattsburg, Pennsylvania, when he saw a bright speck of light appear out of the woods, headed in his direction. The object, which appeared to grow as it approached him, turned out to be a brilliant blue silvery ball about 14 inches in diameter.

The strange object came within four feet of Knight at about eye level, before it looped back around and flew into the woods again, traveling at 35-40 miles per hour. To Knight's amazement, the object reappeared twice more, executing the exact same maneuver as the first time. Knight called his wife, who came out of the house and saw the bluish sphere when it appeared for a third time.

Knight said, "When it had gone, we waited for it to return but it did not come back. Then I asked my wife, 'What did you see?' And she said, 'A ball of light came and went away.'"

Knight added, "I am no scientist but now I am convinced there is a direct relationship between what we saw and the so-called flying saucers."

Some researchers have suggested that Knight and his wife may have merely experienced the phenomenon known as "ball lightning."

In 1935, either on January 22 or 23, at 8 p.m., a woman in Vienna, Virginia, saw a lightning-like flash in the southwest that flared up several times before dying down. The bright flash seemed to come from a "great blazing light, almost a ball of fire," that was moving around the horizon. It was lost to view in the southeast. The incident was reported in *Science* magazine, number 81, in 1935.

In 1936, two amateur astronomers in the Panama Canal Zone, Mrs. E. P. Higgins and a companion, observed an object that appeared to be an "orange-red star" moving from north to south, near Miraflores Lake, Panama. Suddenly, it halted in midair and travelled in three small loops from right to left.

In the fall of 1936, shortly before midnight, Louie R. Lindblad and five companions from Texarkana, Arkansas, were fox hunting in Bowie County, Texas, when they observed numerous starlike objects in a circular formation. Occasionally a light would fly across the circle and take up another position until they all seem to relocate. They watched the display for about 30–40 minutes. The sighting was reported in the August 1980 issue of the *Mutual UFO Network (MUFON) Journal*.

In the early 1950s, mysterious fireballs again made headlines throughout America, particularly in the Southwest, where they were suspected of being some type of secret weapon invented by the Soviet Union. Strange, greenish-tinted fireballs were observed in numerous locations, often near a U.S. military base.

Observations of mysterious fireballs continue even today, remaining as unexplainable as they were in the 1930s and in the 1950s.

Spring-Heeled Jack

HOPPING HUMANOIDS

*Silver City, New Mexico
and the East Coast
1938-1939*

SILVER CITY, NEW MEXICO, is perhaps most famous as being the boyhood home of Billy the Kid. The Boy Bandit King arrived in Silver City with his mother, brother, and stepfather at the tender age of 13. Not long after, Billy's mother would die there, and Billy would begin his descent into a life of crime. As most Western enthusiasts know, he was gunned down at 21 and became a legend of his time. However, Silver City was also paid a visit by another Nineteenth Century sensation—and an otherworldly one at that. That's because in 1938, Silver City was visited by a mysterious humanoid known for incredible feats of acrobatics – Spring-Heeled Jack.

Just exactly who or what is Spring-Heeled Jack, you ask? Spring-Heeled Jack, so named for his ability to leap for long distances, literally sprang onto the Fortean scene in 1830's London. Descriptions of the strange being differed depending upon the witness, but fundamentally Spring Heeled Jack had the shape and appearance of a man. Sometimes the man was tall and thin, other times stocky and burly. Some reports had him wearing a cape with a lamp on his chest, others said he had wings—a few even said that he breathed fire. The common denominator was always that the man-thing could jump significant distances, hence the name Spring-Heeled Jack.

For the year of 1837, the police paid no mind to the sightings for the most part. In February of 1838 came forward a respectable citizen who in all earnestness claimed that his daughter had been terrified by the being. He reported the incident to the police, stating that the previous night his daughter, Jane Alsop, had heard a ring at the gate. Outside, a tall man, shrouded in fog and wearing a cloak, claimed that he was a police officer who had just captured Spring-Heeled Jack. The officer asked her to hurry and get a lantern. When she went out to meet the man, he threw off his cloak revealing a "hideous and frightful appearance". He was wearing some sort of helmet and clad in a tight, shiny white suit (she compared it to "white oilskin"). His hands ended in metallic claws, with which he reached out to the girl, tearing her dress in the process. And to top it all off, he breathed blue and white flames! The girl's screams attracted more townsfolk, and Jack bounded away into the night as he always did.

A few nights later a woman named Lucy Sales was walking along a respectable Limehouse street when she was accosted by the same figure along with her sister. Sales didn't get a good look at the figure because as soon as she saw it, it breathed "a quantity of blue flame" in the direction of her face. The flame blinded her briefly thereafter and she collapsed to the ground as her sister came to her side and Jack merely walked away.

A FLYING MACHINE.

WHAT TWO LOUISVILLIANS SAW LAST EVENING.

Between 6 and 7 o'clock last evening while Messrs. C. A. Youngman and Ben Flexner were standing at a side window of Haddart's drug store, at Second and Chestnut streets, looking skyward, they discovered an object high up in the air apparently immediately above the Ohio river bridge, which they at first thought was the wreck of a toy balloon. As it got nearer they observed that it had the appearance of a man surrounded by machinery, which he seemed to be working with his feet and hands. He worked his feet as though he was running a treadle, and his arms seemed to be swinging to and fro above his head, though the latter movement sometimes appeared to be executed with wings or fans. The gazers became considerably worked up by the apparition, and inspected it very closely. They could see the delicate outlines of machinery, but the object was too high up to make out its exact construction.

The Courier-Journal (Louisville, Kentucky), 7-29-1880, p. 4

A fire breathing man with metal claws wearing a helmet with a shiny jumpsuit? If this doesn't sound like a B-movie alien, nothing does, and yet it was reported all the way back in the 1830s. Due to his strange appearance, writers in the 1950s began to speculate that perhaps Jack was an alien of some sort. One went as far as to speculate Jack came from a planet with high gravity, hence his ability to bound through Earth's with ease.

The theory that Jack was some kind of E.T. might gain momentum by way of an 1880 sighting all the way over in Louisville, Kentucky. In July of that year the fiend was spotted leaping around Old Louisville. Like the other Spring-Heeled Jack, this figure was tall, thin, wore a jumpsuit and helmet and had a lamp on his chest. He also tore at several women's dresses and performed high leaps and bounds. The creature was reported within the town boundaries (jumping over a horse drawn carriage no less!) and also at outlying farms where he was seen leaping over a haystack! A few weeks later, a strange humanoid was spotted operating some kind of aerial vehicle not unlike a gyrocopter.

One hundred years later, a new Spring Heeled Jack sighting surfaced in a 1980 letter written to the Center for UFO Studies. It related the sighting of four children in Silver City, New Mexico, in the twilight hours in the summer of 1938. The witnesses' name was Ann Alley, and her letter was reprinted in Jerome Clark's book *The Unexplained*:

Vintage Postcard of Silver City, NM

We all saw him. He was dressed all in gray and he even seemed gray; he was drifting or floating at tree-top level. The thing I remember the most about him was that he seemed to be wearing a belt which was wide and had points sticking out of it. He also seemed to be wearing a cape (a la Flash Gordon).

He drifted across the sky above us and we all stood and stared, speechless. It did not occur to us to question this phenomena [sic]; as children we accepted it....

About fifteen years ago I was telling my husband about it. When I did, I questioned myself—perhaps I had had a dream. But just in case, I called my brother. By now I was about thirty-five and he about thirty-two. I prefaced my conversation by telling him that I had a strange story to tell and that perhaps it had all been a dream, but that I thought that in about 1938 I had seen a man fly over our heads. He stopped me and said, "It wasn't a dream." He went on to describe everything as I have described it here, including the belt and the cape.

Silver City in 1938

While this may not have been the original Spring-Heeled Jack, it was certainly a similar creature or being. It's also interesting that this sighting took place one hundred years after Spring Heeled Jack was last seen in London in 1838. Furthermore, Silver City wasn't the only place a Spring Heeled Jack-type being was sighted in the late 1930s. Preceding this sighting was a trio of floating humanoids seen in the skies of Palm Springs, California, in July of 1936. The information is scarce, not to mention a little dubious since it came courtesy of Gray Barker, a notorious hoaxer. The report stated that three helmeted humanoids were floating over the area, somewhat similar to the Silver City entity. However, while there's not much to go on with the Palm Beach and Silver City sightings, later a true successor to Spring Heeled Jack would appear on the East Coast of the United States.

The first reports began to come in mid-October of 1939 when frightened school children came home to report having been attacked by a monster. Judging from their descriptions of a big, black something leaping out to frighten them, parents paid the children's accounts little mind. In the second week of November, a woman in Provincetown named Maria Costa claimed to have been accosted by a man with a "black hood, black cape, black face" with "fierce eyes and long pointed ears [that] were a glowing silver." Costa fled to a nearby coffee shop screaming. Catching the attention of the men inside, they were inclined to run out and try to chase down Costa's attacker, but it was already gone. Later, Costa gave a statement to the police and claimed that the man was huge, nearly eight feet tall and made a strange "loud buzzing sound" that reminded her of "a June bug on a hot day, only louder." And her last detail of significance: "He disappeared like a flash." Thanks to that end statement, the being was eventually nicknamed the Black Flash (though the Provincetown Phantom and the Devil of the Dunes was also considered).

Over the next three weeks, more encounters ensued. Four other witnesses sighted the being in downtown Provincetown, where the Black Flash dropped out of trees or from rooftops. At least two of the witnesses were husky, well-built men who found the Black Flash quite frightening. One man who was chased by the fiend reported that he was no match for the Black Flash's speed and agility.

Black Flash in Old Provincetown Says 'Booh,' and Are Folks Scared!

Special Dispatch to the Globe

PROVINCETOWN, Oct. 23—This resort town, which manages to keep in the public eye even after the artists leave for a warmer clime in the Fall, has a new What-Is-It in the form of a hooded figure which prowls the streets at night.

Never at a loss for a name, the natives have christened their newest weird visitor, the "Black Flash," although a few still hold out for the shorter title, the "Blot." Nobody has seen the thing's face; but a couple of boys, who claim they met the apparition head-on, say it has a mouth and speaks in a guttural tongue.

Police remain adamant about tackling the Black Flash, philosophically declaring they "officially" don't recognize its existence, and won't—at least until they can pin something definite on it. In fact, there is a belief among some of the members of the department that the Flash has

some premature connection with Halloween.

Meanwhile the mystery remains as mysterious as ever. Two terrified youths raced 15 blocks into the lighted center of the town in the small hours of this morning after they claim the Flash rushed out of an alley at them yelling "Boo! Boo!" They said their attacker was seven feet tall and wore a black hood and long black cape.

A somewhat similar description was given by an elderly lady who lives on Bangs st. She reported seeing the Flash on one of the window sills of her home. Her cries, she said, drove it away.

Stories of the Flash have circulated here almost every Fall for the past eight years. About four years ago it was blamed for setting a string of fires which resulted in more than $250,000 worth of damage to property.

The natives say the Flash will go away by itself after Oct. 31.

The sightings intensified as one night local police surrounded the phantom in a schoolyard. Shining their flashlights on the being's face, in their opinion, the police thought the humanoid was wearing "a mask, which looked like an old flour-screen without its handle, painted silver and strapped to the phantom's head."

Though the fence encompassing the yard was ten feet tall, the Black Flash leapt over it. As if this wasn't spring-heeled enough, soon after a teenager claimed that the Black Flash shot blue flames at his face! Not long after this, a farmer encountered the monstrous man. He fired his rifle at the Black Flash, which merely laughed at him then bounded away over an eight-foot hedge.

Unfortunately, many of these fantastic accounts can't be traced back to actual newspapers, and instead are mostly oral histories collected by a local historian named Robert Ellis Cahill, who published the tales in *New England's Mad and Mysterious Men* in 1984.

Postcard of Provincetown C.1939.

However, in more recent years, a determined researcher named Theo Paijmans found at least one newspaper account from the *Provincetown Advocate* dated October 26, 1939. Unfortunately for forteans, the newspaper neglects to mention any of the Black Flash's more fanciful attributes, and apparently just names the phantom as a strange, leaping man. The most noteworthy portions of the paper simply stated that the fiend was fond of "...grabbing women, jumping over ten foot hedges with no trouble at all." The paper also claimed that "Chair springs on his feet" as the simple explanation. Furthermore, the piece was titled "Fall Brings Out The 'Black Flash'" with the sub-headline, "Hard Winter Certain As 'Cabin Fever' Stories Start."

In that same article, the current chief of police, Anthony Tarvers, theorized it was two teenagers in a trench coat, with one standing on the other's shoulders to boost their height.

Further demystifying the leaper are comments made by Provincetown's Police Chief Francis Marshall in 1959 to Cahill. He claimed he knew the name, or rather names, of the Black Flash, but would not divulge them:

> I will tell you this though... The Black Flash wasn't just one person. He was four men, who sometimes played the part alone, and sometimes together. Two are dead now, but the others have a hell of a time when they get together, reminiscing about the times they scared the hell out of their friends and neighbors in Provincetown.

Is this the mundane reality of the Black Flash? Or, were old men simply having a fun time by claiming they were the leaping humanoid. Afterall, copycats do happen. The authors have met individuals who claimed to play a part in UFO encounters when they in fact did not, and were just jovial old men indulging in a joke. [This is no fun for ufologists though, as people like this always muddy the waters.]

As it stands, it seems too much that the Black Flash had so much in common with Spring-Heeled Jack, long forgotten by the late 1930s, especially in America (don't forget, the first flap of Jack sightings were all in England). Furthermore, O'Donnell Heights, Maryland, was terrorized by a similar creature at exactly the same time. It was reported as a tall, thin "prowler" dressed in all black who could make extreme leaps and bounds.

Twenty years earlier, Nassau County in Long Island, New York, suffered a flap of sightings of a strange being that could have been called the Long Island Leaper, though newspapers of the time compared the being to Dracula and alleged that he nested in trees.

With so many leaping, fire-breathing humanoids spotted over the years, it stands to reason that the Black Flash might well have been part of the Spring-Heeled Jack family despite claims that the being was really just a few ornery teenagers. Because, just as hoaxers muddy the waters of UFO and alien encounters, so too do skeptics that are all too eager to explain away strange occurrences...

The Cover of Menger's Book.

CONTACTEES OF THE 1930S

Nationwide, 1930s

THOUGH THE TERM "CONTACTEE" was not used until the 1950s, the phenomenon has its roots in the 1930s. But before we get into that, we should define what a contactee is. First, there is a significant difference between an alien abductee and a contactee. Whereas an abductee suffers what is usually perceived as a negative experience, a contactee engages in communication with the aliens and views the experience as positive.

In 1972's *The UFO Experience: A Scientific Inquiry*, J. Allen Hynek defined the contactee phenomenon as

> ...the visitation to the earth of generally benign beings whose ostensible purpose is to

communicate (generally to a relatively few selected and favored persons) messages of "cosmic importance". These chosen recipients generally have repeated contact experiences, involving additional messages.

However, although Hynek acknowledged the phenomenon, that didn't mean that he and other ufologists believed in the rather far-out claims of many contactees. As it stands, many contactees managed to profit from their alleged E.T. encounters via books and media. Some even cultivated followers.

One of the better known contactees to emerge in the 1950s was Howard Menger, who had his first contactee experience back in 1932 near High Bridge, New Jersey. Menger was ten years old and spending his afternoon in a quiet wooded area, when he encountered "the most exquisite woman he had ever seen" sitting on a rock. The woman not only had golden hair but golden eyes as well. She wore a shiny nylon-like seamless outfit and told Menger, "I have come a long way to see you, Howard...and talk to you."

Menger would later recollect that the unearthly woman knew much not only about his past, but his future and "what my purpose would be on Earth." She also told him that her people had been observing him for quite a while and that they were "contacting their own"—implying Menger was himself in some way alien. Most startling of all, the woman answered Menger's questions before he could ask them out loud. Before departing, she told Menger that they would meet again and also warned of future wars and destruction.

Later, Menger wrote a whole book based around this encounter entitled *From Outer Space to You.* In his books, Menger expressed the belief that these benevolent aliens hailed from Venus, though in later years he would backtrack on this theory. Today, Menger's credibility is all but ruined due to his conflicting claims. For instance, for a time in the late 1960s, he alleged that his alien encounters were really government orchestrated smokescreen operations. Later, he backtracked to the belief that the beings were actual aliens.

In any case, Menger wasn't the only contactee of the 1930s. The same year that Menger had his first encounter, so too did two brothers near Killdeer, North Dakota. According to the account, one evening Leo Dworshak and his brother Michael were playing in a lonely, rural area when they saw a UFO. They said that it had flashing colored lights circling it in a band, and that it rotated "in a complicated way." It landed, and when the boys went closer to investigate, they said that the craft had "an invisible force field" around it that kept them from getting too close to it.

As the ship rose away and departed, they noticed that it produced neither sound nor exhaust fumes. The next night the ship and its occupants returned. This time, the aliens—which the boys described as looking like twin humans—invited the brothers on board their craft. The beings disinfected the boys and once they stepped inside gave them a tour of the ship. Inside the craft, Dworshak recalled that the aliens could move chairs with their minds. They were also told that the ship had a force field that could turn it invisible when need be. Then, they told them of things to come including the invention of the home computer and the imminent rise of the Nazis. Lastly, they told the brothers that they came from the "12th galaxy" and that they kept "12 of their kind on earth at all times."

While this story is no doubt interesting, it wasn't divulged until 2003 to reporter Martin Kidston of the *Independent Record* of Helena, Montana. Had the boys actually divulged all of this at the time, then the alien's prediction of the home computer and the Nazi party would have been more eyebrow raising. But, as it is now, it's too easy to conclude that Dworshak made it all up.

Contactee cases were relatively quiet for the rest of the decade up until 1939. In June of that year in California, a notorious contactee named Dana Howard claimed to have had her first E.T. experience. Though Howard wouldn't divulge her claim until it was fashionable in the 1950s, she said that she met a beautiful Venusian girl named Diane. Over the years she would have several encounters with Venusians, who offered to take her to Venus and so on. As stated in our introduction to this chapter, Howard is among the contactees to profit from her experiences via books.

Slightly more interesting, but nonetheless still dubious, was another contactee story from the following month, in July. A fortune teller in rural Alabama had landed herself on the government radar when she began divulging military secrets.

This warranted a visit from the FBI, who went to pay the woman a visit. They found her sitting on the front porch of her home as though she were waiting for them. They stated the purpose of their visit and told her they had some questions for her. She politely informed the men that she wasn't actually a fortuneteller, but a "mind reader" who hailed from "another world"! The agents played along and asked her what her purpose was on Earth, and she told them that she was "guarding something that did not concern humans."

The agents stated that they wished to take her in for questioning, but she informed the men that she would not go with them. When one of the agents ascended her porch steps to apprehend her, he began to tremble and fell to the ground. She informed the men that if they wished to depart with their lives, they had better not touch her. According to the far-out story, the agents obliged, but also asked for further proof of her alien lineage before they left.

The woman told the men to have their superiors pick a 100 square mile track of land and put markers around it. After this, no airplanes were to fly over the area. Oddly enough, when the agents told their superiors of this, they did as the woman asked and cordoned off some land. When they later inspected the cordoned off land, they found that it was now completely devoid of animal and plant life! Why and how did this happen? Did the woman's alien benefactors pick it clean? We don't know, nor does the story elaborate, it simply ends there.

The story is severely lacking in credibility, obviously, and comes from an unverified publication cited as *UFOs In New Mexico & The World*. No one is certain if this source is a book, an article, a documentary, or something else. In any case, it's a dubious capper to a chapter filled with a lot of dubious claims.

DULCE'S
FIRST UFOS

Dulce, New Mexico
Late 1930s

DULCE, NEW MEXICO, will always be one of the more notorious hotspots for UFO activity. We use the term notorious because the accounts to spring from Dulce are among ufology's most far out stories. For those unaware, Dulce is a Jicarilla Apache Reservation in northern New Mexico, in Rio Arriba County bordering Colorado. Dulce's population is quite low at just a little over 2,000 people. However, that's just above ground. Like Area 51 in Nevada, under the area's Archuleta Mesa is rumored to be a secret U.S. military base related to extraterrestrial technology. Actually, unlike Area 51, controlled by the U.S. military,

Dulce's base is supposedly a joint custody base between humans and extraterrestrials.

As we stated before, the area is a hotbed of UFO activity running the gamut of typical flying saucer sightings to cattle mutilations. Dulce's best remembered story is an account dating back to 1979, which alleged that a firefight occurred between humans and aliens in the base. The story sprang from Phil Schneider, who claimed to be a former government engineer who helped construct the secret base under the mesa. According to Schneider, during the underground construction work they ran into a group of tall Grey aliens and a firefight ensued between the beings and the U.S. military. Long story short, a peace treaty was eventually established, hence the joint human-alien base. See why we said Dulce was notorious? [However, that said, Schneider very mysteriously, cough—conveniently—cough, died via suicide in 1996 only one year after telling his story.]

Whether the 1979 story is true or not, the Dulce area is, for a fact, an area where a great deal of UFO activity takes place—even back during the era of the Great Depression. Though the Jicarilla Apache Reservation had been established back in the 1880s, under the Indian Reorganization Act of 1934, the tribe became more self-sufficient, acquiring more land and livestock. [Today, it owns and operates its own oil and gas wells.] A few years later, in either 1938 or 1939, occurred what was quite possibly Dulce's first UFO. It was during that time period that Manuel Gomez remembered seeing a bright, green fireball streak across the skies over Dulce. [Gomez couldn't remember the exact year and cited it as 1938 or 1939.] That we know of, author Jack Kutz was the first to publish this heretofore unknown account in his book *More Mysteries and Miracles of New Mexico.* Kutz wrote that Gomez related that, "[The green fireball] had come sailing over the tree tops, 'hissing like a snake' one evening just after sunset." [Kutz, p.208]

Painting of Green Fireball
by Mrs. Lincoln La Paz.

This green fireball sighting preceded a whole flap of green fireballs that streaked over the skies of New Mexico exactly ten years later throughout 1948 and 1949. The array of green fireballs filling the skies so puzzled the U.S. military that they launched an official investigation into the phenomenon headed by Dr. Lincoln La Paz. The fireballs were a great cause for concern for the military, and on January 13, 1949, the Director of Army Intelligence from Fourth Army

Headquarters in Texas wrote that the green fireballs "[may be] the result of radiological warfare experiments by a foreign power." He added that the fireballs were "of such great importance, especially as they are occurring in the vicinity of sensitive installations, that a scientific board [should]...study the situation."

That a green fireball passed over Dulce ten years earlier, and many years before the alleged underground base was constructed, is fascinating. And that wasn't the only old time Dulce UFO encounter recorded by Kutz in *More Mysteries and Miracles of New Mexico*. He also spoke to one of Dulce's oldest residents in the 1980s, Helen Vicente, who herself saw a UFO when she was a young woman. Unfortunately, she did not give the exact year, but it could have been within this book's time period. All she said was that a disc passed overhead one day as she walked to church. She also told Kutz that her brothers were riding horses on Archueletta Mesa one day when a UFO buzzed them. They described it as a silver disc that passed so closely that it greatly disturbed their horses, which nearly threw the men off.

Don't forget, Archuleta Mesa is precisely the spot where the underground base was constructed in the late 1970s. And as bizarre as stories coming from Dulce are, the accounts of Vicente and her family would seem to back up the claims that there was an alien presence in the area long before the U.S. military allegedly chose Archuleta Mesa as a base.

AFTERWORD

WITH THE DAWNING OF THE 1940s began the modern era of Unidentified Flying Objects, kicked off by sightings of mysterious "foo fighters" by pilots during the early part of World War II. The decade was bookmarked by two reported UFO crashes – one in Cape Girardeau, Missouri, in 1941, and the more famous one in 1947, in the desert north of Roswell, New Mexico. 1942 was the year of the famous "Battle of Los Angeles," during which U.S. antiaircraft artillery fired hundreds of rounds into the air after the reported sighting of multiple UFOs off the coast of California.

The modern UFO era, generally said to have begun in the 1940s, has been covered in literally thousands of books over the years, and we the authors made a conscious decision early in this series to end our research for our books with the year 1939. The reason we end our series where most books begin is obvious – our purpose was to show that significant UFO sightings and encounters occurred in North America long before 1940, which is why we began our books with accounts of UFOs from the 1800s. Thus, our very first foray into this topic, a little book titled *The Real Cowboys & Aliens: UFO Encounters of the Old West*, achieved great notoriety and success, prompting us to begin the current series that has provided exhaustive coverage of UFO sightings beginning in the year 1800 and concluding in the year 1939.

While we end this particular series, we already have several new series in the works having to do with other strange phenomena of the same time period. We continue to believe that this era has been woefully overlooked in the past in books written about paranormal occurrences in North America, and it is our intention to focus in on these strange, unexplained events of the past in our future series.

And with that dear reader, we bring to a close our look at UFO sightings from 1800 to 1939. It is our sincere hope that you have enjoyed going on this wonderous journey along with us.

INDEX

ABOUT THE AUTHOR

A recognized expert in the field of UFOs and the paranormal, Noe Torres is an author, publisher, and former Texas state section director for the Mutual UFO Network (MUFON). He holds a Bachelor's in English and a Master's in Library Science from the University of Texas at Austin. He has written one of the most popular books about the famous Roswell Incident, titled *Ultimate Guide to the Roswell UFO Crash*, which is among the top selling books at gift shops in Roswell, New Mexico. Torres also co-wrote with Roswell, New Mexico, historian John LeMay the critically-acclaimed book *The Real Cowboys & Aliens: UFO Encounters of the Old West* in 2011, which was followed by a series of books on the same theme: *The Real Cowboys & Aliens: Early American UFOs*, *The Real Cowboys & Aliens: Old West UFOs*, *The Real Cowboys & Aliens: The Coming of the Airships*, *The Real Cowboys & Aliens: The Lost Cases*, *Early 20th Century UFOs*, and *UFOs in the Roaring Twenties*. In addition, Torres has authored or co-authored a number of other well-reviewed books, including *Mexico's Roswell*, *The Other Roswell*, *Aliens in the Forest*, *Fallen Angel*, and *The Coyame Incident*.

Torres has appeared on several nationally-broadcast television shows, including season 2, episode 5 of the Travel Channel series *UFO Witness* titled "Grey Alien-Human Hybridization," in which he talks about UFO witnesses who have been injured or killed during encounters with UFO entities. He also appeared in season 2, episode 1 of the Travel Channel's *Mysteries of the Outdoors*, titled "Strange Attraction." In that show, he is interviewed extensively about unexplained mysteries in Big Bend National Park. Also in 2017, Noe was featured in an episode titled "The Marfa Lights" for the TV series *Mysteries of the Unexplained.* In 2008, he appeared in season 1, episode 4 of the History Channel's *UFO Hunters*, in a show called "Crash and Retrieval."

Torres has appeared several times on George Noory's famous radio show Coast to Coast AM, as well as on The Jeff Rense Program and many other shows. He is also in high demand as a speaker at UFO and paranormal conferences and festivals, having been a featured speaker at the 2017 International UFO Congress in Scottsdale, Arizona. He has also spoken five times at the annual Roswell UFO Conference and at many other UFO conferences throughout the United States and Mexico. He makes frequent appearances as a guest speaker in person and by video conferencing at paranormal conferences throughout the United States.

In addition, Torres has founded a number of UFO conferences throughout Texas, including the Laredo UFO Conference, the Del Rio UFO Festival, the Presidio UFO Festival, and the Edinburg UFO Conference & Festival, which was recently ranked by ListVerse.com as the #3 best UFO festival in the world. His efforts to organize UFO conferences in Texas were spotlighted by

Texas Observer magazine in the article "Aliens Without Borders: Exploring Texas' Intergalactic Attractions" (June 11, 2014).

ABOUT THE AUTHOR

John LeMay was born and raised in Roswell, NM, the "UFO Capital of the World." He is the author of over 40 books on film and western history such as *Kong Unmade: The Lost Films of Skull Island*, *Tall Tales and Half Truths of Billy the Kid*, *Roswell USA: Towns That Celebrate UFOs, Lake Monsters, Bigfoot and Other Weirdness* and the western novels *The Noted Desperado Pancho Dumez* and *Once Upon a Time in Fort Sumner*. He is the editor/publisher of both *The Lost Films Fanzine, Strange West Magazine,* and has written for magazines such as *True West, Cinema Retro,* and *Mad Scientist* to name only a few. He is a Past President of the Board of Directors for the Historical Society for Southeast New Mexico.

ALSO AVAILABLE

CRYPTOZOOLOGY/COWBOYS & SAURIANS

Cowboys & Saurians: Prehistoric Beasts as Seen by the Pioneers explores dinosaur sightings from the pioneer period via real newspaper reports from the time. Well-known cases like the Tombstone Thunderbird are covered along with more obscure cases like the Crosswicks Monster and more. Softcover (357 pp/5.06" X 7.8") Suggested Retail: $19.95 ISBN: 978-1-7341546-1-0

Cowboys & Saurians: Ice Age zeroes in on snowbound saurians like the Ceratosaurus of the Arctic Circle and a Tyrannosaurus of the Tundra, as well as sightings of Ice Age megafauna like mammoths, glyptodonts, Sarkastodons and Saber-toothed tigers. Tales of a land that time forgot in the Arctic are also covered. Softcover (264 pp/5.06" X 7.8") Suggested Retail: $14.99 ISBN: 978-1-7341546-7-2

Southerners & Saurians takes the series formula of exploring newspaper accounts of monsters in the pioneer period with an eye to the Old South. In addition to dinosaurs are covered Lizardmen, Frogmen, giant leeches and mosquitoes, and the Dingocroc, which might be an alien rather than a prehistoric survivor. Softcover (202 pp/5.06" X 7.8") Suggested Retail: $13.99 ISBN: 978-1-7344730-4-9

Cowboys & Saurians South of the Border explores the saurians of Central and South America, like the Patagonian Plesiosaurus that was really an Iemisch, plus tales of the Neo-Mylodon, a menacing monster from underground called the Minhocao, Glyptodonts, and even Bolivia's three-headed dinosaur! Softcover (412 pp/5.06"X7.8") Suggested Retail: $17.95 ISBN: 978-1-953221-73-5

UFOLOGY/THE REAL COWBOYS & ALIENS IN CONJUNCTION WITH ROSWELL BOOKS

The Real Cowboys and Aliens: Early American UFOs explores UFO sightings in the USA between the years 1800-1864. Stories of encounters sometimes involved famous figures in U.S. history such as Lewis and Clark, and Thomas Jefferson.Hardcover (242pp/6" X 9") Softcover (262 pp/5.06" X 7.8") Suggested Retail: $24.99 (hc)/$15.95(sc) ISBN: 978-1-7341546-8-9\(hc)/978-1-7344730-8-7(sc)

The second entry in the series, *Old West UFOs*, covers reports spanning the years 1865-1895. Includes tales of Men in Black, Reptilians, Spring-Heeled Jack, Sasquatch from space, and other alien beings, in addition to the UFOs and airships. Hardcover (276 pp/6" X 9") Softcover (308 pp/5.06" X 7.8") Suggested Retail: $29.95 (hc)/$17.95(sc) ISBN: 978-1-7344730-0-1 (hc)/ 978-1-73447 30-2-5 (sc)

The third entry in the series, *The Coming of the Airships*, encompasses a short time frame with an incredibly high concentration of airship sightings between 1896-1899. The famous Aurora, Texas, UFO crash of 1897 is covered in depth along with many others. Hardcover (196 pp/6" X 9") Softcover (222 pp/5.06" X 7.8") Suggested Retail: $24.99 (hc)/$15.95(sc) ISBN: 978-1-7347816 -1-8 (hc)/978-1-7347816-0-1(sc)

Early 20th Century UFOs kicks off a new series that investigates UFO sightings of the early 1900s. Includes tales of UFOs sighted over the *Titanic* as it sunk, Nikola Tesla receiving messages from the stars, an alien being found encased in ice, and a possible virus from outer space!Hardcover (196 pp/6" X 9") Softcover (222 pp/5.06" X 9") Suggested Retail: $27.99 (hc)/$16.95(sc) ISBN: 978-1-7347816-1-8 (hc)/978-1-73478 16-0-1(sc)